"Larry Brooks tells it like it is! If your g
and garners great reviews, you need to ⌐
es and absorbing the insightful analysis and astute advice. Then read it through again, using Brooks's gems of wisdom and case studies to amp up your premise, plot, and characters and hone your storytelling skills." —Jodie Renner, editor and award-winning author of *Fire up Your Fiction*, *Captivate Your Readers*, and *Writing a Killer Thriller*

"In a marketplace filled with rehashed, often oversimplified advice, Brooks pulls no punches. Larry speaks to you like the professional writer he *knows* you can become. He clearly understands the difference between what you may want to hear—and what you *need* to hear." —Art Holcomb, award-winning writer and educator

"Writing the novel is half the battle. The other half is fixing it. In this book, master craftsman Larry Brooks gives you his set of tools for the fix-it stage. So strap on your belt, and get to work! —James Scott Bell, author of *Write Great Fiction: Plot & Structure*

"Larry Brooks has scoured, explored, and unearthed the elements of unforgettable fiction and set the entire treasure at our feet. Not only will *Story Fix* take your writing to the next level, but it will create a better understanding of the writer's mind and how we can be proactive where story is concerned." —Heather Burch, best-selling author of *One Lavender Ribbon* and *Along the Broken Road*

"Larry Brooks is, simply stated, a great thinker about story form. You'll get so much from his advice and mentorship." —Jennifer Lauck, *New York Times* best-selling author of *Blackbird*, *Still Waters*, *Show Me the Way*, and *Found*

"*Story Fix* is an essential diagnostic tool for writers. Larry Brooks shows the reader how to perform a 'stress test' on a manuscript or story idea to flush out flaws and weaknesses. *Story Fix* helped me spot a fundamental flaw in the setup of my current project. I went back and reworked the entire concept." —Kathryn Lilley, mystery author and founder of *The Kill Zone* blog

"A few hours reading Larry Brooks on writing is worth fifty hours of normal writing instruction. The only thing better than reading Larry's books is reading his books and sitting in his seminars." —Eric Witchey, award-winning author and instructor

"Hemingway famously said that the only writing is rewriting. But here's the catch: Revision is the hardest part of writing a novel. It requires knowledge, distance, endurance, and vision. This is where *Story Fix* comes in with its brilliance, simplicity, and depth. It will help you repair a shaky premise, weak characterization, or any of the many weaknesses that can doom fiction." —Jessica Page Morrell, author of *Between the Lines* and *Writing Out the Storm*

"*Story Fix* has something for everyone who wants to improve their craft. Whether you're a new writer hoping to break into the business or a more seasoned author struggling with your current project, this book will help you take it to the next level."
—Chevy Stevens, *New York Times* best-selling author

"*Story Fix* is the book that will take you to the mountaintop. What awaits is an exhilarating ride into your best story. Hang on!" —Kay Kenyon, acclaimed fantasy and science fiction author

"Okay, so you knock off a 100,000-word novel you think is a masterpiece, but by the sour look on your best friend's mug when he or she reads it, you know it's crap and you face the awful truth that you have to rewrite. You then discover the agony of rewriting and find that it's sort of like whacking yourself in the head with a crowbar ten hours a day. So you stumble through a few hundred rewrites before you realize that you don't really know *how* to rewrite, and that what you're producing is a long string of first drafts, each one as bad as the last. What to do? You can turn to single malt scotch, fill your backpack with rocks and jump in deep water, or you can learn to master the art of rewriting by diligently studying and applying the principles you'll find in *Story Fix*." —James N. Frey, internationally acclaimed creative writing teacher and author of *How to Write a Damn Good Novel*

"The revision process is where *New York Times* bestsellers are born. To achieve success, a writer needs tools. The good news is that, finally, there's a how-to guide written by a pro who helps writers bridge the gap from 'It sucks' to 'It's great.'" —Mindy Halleck, award-winning writer, novelist, and writing instructor (www.MindyHalleck.com)

"I have the pleasure of teaming up with Larry Brooks on *The Kill Zone*, one of the best resources for writers of thrillers and mysteries. I've discovered that Larry's advice to aspiring novelists is straightforward, clear-eyed, and best of all, full of empathy. Larry knows you can't write a publishable novel without a lot of hard work, and he's not afraid to say it. I recommend *Story Fix* to anyone who's truly serious about writing fiction."
—Mark Alpert, internationally best-selling author of *The Six* and *The Orion Plan*

"No matter what level of writing you've reached, *Story Fix* is the ultimate road map into understanding what it takes to piece together your own success. Larry Brooks delivers an incredible guide that will help you redefine the heartbeat of existing talents. Fix more than your story—fix your approach!" —Delilah Marvelle, *USA Today* best-selling author

"Brilliance. Clarity. Heart. That's what you'll bring to your story (and storytelling education) after reading this book. Whether you're starting a new story or fixing an old one that isn't working, there's something for every writer here on these pages. I'm a story coach by profession, and I still learned a ton. —Jennifer Blanchard, author and story coach (www.JenniferBlanchard.net)

STORY
FIX

TRANSFORM YOUR NOVEL
FROM BROKEN TO BRILLIANT

LARRY BROOKS

FOREWORD BY MICHAEL HAUGE

WRITER'S DIGEST
BOOKS

WritersDigest.*com*
Cincinnati, Ohio

For more resources for writers, visit www.writersdigest.com.

19 18 17 16 15   5 4 3 2 1

Distributed in Canada by Fraser Direct
100 Armstrong Avenue
Georgetown, Ontario, Canada L7G 5S4
Tel: (905) 877-4411

Distributed in the U.K. and Europe by F&W Media International
Brunel House, Newton Abbot, Devon, TQ12 4PU, England
Tel: (+44) 1626-323200, Fax: (+44) 1626-323319
E-mail: postmaster@davidandcharles.co.uk

Distributed in Australia by Capricorn Link
P.O. Box 704, Windsor, NSW 2756 Australia
Tel: (02) 4577-3555

ISBN13: 978-1-59963-911-6

EDITED BY Rachel Randall
DESIGNED BY Alexis Brown
PRODUCTION COORDINATED BY Debbie Thomas

DEDICATION

For Laura, for always.

ACKNOWLEDGMENTS

No author is alone with his work, which is a good thing for writers and readers alike. I'd like to thank Phil Sexton and the team at F+W and Writer's Digest Books for their steadfast support and consistently stellar design work, with special thanks to Rachel Randall for the incredible value-add imbued by her editing, vision, and advocacy. Thanks to Art Holcomb for modeling what a real pro looks like in this business, and for the inspiration while having my back. And thanks to Joel Canfield for his big brain and willingness to help, to Jim Frey for the best book blurb ever, and to the many Storyfix.com writer-readers who keep me motivated and in the right lane as I balance teaching and coaching work with my own fiction and nonfiction projects.

ABOUT THE AUTHOR

Larry Brooks is the author of three books on writing fiction, including the bestseller *Story Engineering: Mastering the Six Core Competencies of Successful Writing* and the award-winning *Story Physics: Harnessing the Underlying Forces of Storytelling*. He is also the *USA Today* best-selling author of six critically acclaimed thrillers and the creator of the award-winning website Storyfix.com, named six years running by *Writer's Digest* magazine in their annual "101 Best Websites for Writers" list. Brooks lives in Scottsdale, Arizona, and travels frequently as a speaker and workshop teacher at conferences and at the behest of writing groups who like their instruction served hot and straight up.

TABLE OF **CONTENTS**

PART ONE
The Raw Grist of Story Fixing

PART TWO
Repair

PART THREE
Resurrection

PART FOUR
Redemption

"Nobody knows anything."

—WILLIAM GOLDMAN, NOVELIST,
PLAYWRIGHT, AND SCREENWRITER

FOREWORD

My mentor Art Arthur, who was a screenwriter for more than forty years, said that an essential principle of good writing was this: *Don't get it right; get it written.* If you strive to reach perfection, you'll never even get to good. So let that first draft be too long, too wordy, too dialogue heavy, and too meandering. Get all your ideas down, and *then* start the process of editing.

But this raises a new, critical question: *Edit it how?*

How do you turn that avalanche of words and ideas into a novel or screenplay that is unique, emotionally gripping, and commercially viable? How do you know if it's even a story worth telling? *And what do you do next?*

These are the questions Larry Brooks answers—brilliantly—in this book.

But before I talk about *how* Larry does this, here is something you should understand: *Writing a foreword is hard.* Not as hard as writing a novel or a screenplay, certainly. But definitely harder than a postcard, a tweet, or a grocery list.

When asked to write a foreword, you feel honored, elated, and mercenary. *Someone wants me to contribute to his book! He must really like my work. He must think I have a good reputation, or even a following. And now everyone will see my name—maybe even on the cover. They'll think I'm some kind of expert, or else why would I have been asked? They'll Google me and they'll flock to my website and they'll buy all my products and they'll fill all my lectures and they'll line up for coaching. I'll be a household name!* So immediately you answer, "*Yes!* I'd *love* to write the foreword!"

And then a new voice takes over: *Wait a minute. Now I have to write something brilliant—or at least clever. That means I'll actually have to read the book. But what if it isn't any good? Or worse, what if the book is great? What if it's better than my own books? Will I modify my praise? Will I steal the best ideas? And if I do, will I get away with it?*

"Don't worry," I tell myself. "You don't have to read *all* of Larry's book, just enough to say something complimentary. The table of contents and a couple of chapters should give you plenty of ideas. You can knock that off in less than a day."

But here's where my plan turns to disaster. Because once I begin reading, I can't stop. Quite simply, this book is brilliant. So now I'm left with only a day or so to create a foreword that will somehow convince every novelist and screenwriter, and everyone who dreams of being one, that they have to read this book—and use it.

And so, faced with such a huge task and such a harsh deadline, I do what any good, professional writer would do: I roll up my sleeves, sit down at my computer, and ask for an extension.

This foreword is my attempt to convey the value, the inspiration, and the fun you will have following Larry on a journey into the heart of great fiction. In simple, powerful language, Larry transforms the process of rewriting from a discouraging, perfunctory exercise into an art form. He shows you, step by step, how to take your story from weak to strong, from good to great, and from one destined for rejection to one that's likely to get you an agent or a deal.

He does this by providing you with questions that force you to honestly and courageously evaluate your script or manuscript at its foundation. Questions like *What is my concept? What is my premise? What is my theme? What is the dramatic tension?* Larry presents twelve such story elements and essences and asks you to repeatedly grade your understanding of these ideas and your story's success in using them effectively.

And then Larry asks you to confront the most important question of all: *Is my story worth telling?*

This is a question you rarely hear in writing groups or classes, where the guiding belief is usually, "Any story can be saved." Even consultants like myself have a hard time asking this question of clients, for fear of further discouraging or defeating a writer already beaten down by rejection and self-doubt.

But Larry asks you to face the question head on. He shows you how it can lead to valuable learning, greater skill, and ultimately a better story—one that is far more likely to move your career to the level of success you dream of. Larry strips any sugarcoating and false optimism from what it means to be a professional writer, and he reveals the harsh realities of just how much hard work is demanded of you. But he does this in a way that empowers you as a writer and makes you even more excited about the possibilities of your chosen career.

After laying out the questions that ensure a brutally honest evaluation of your story outline, script, or manuscript, he then presents you with the tools and skills to correct those weaknesses and take your story to a whole new level of emotional and commercial potential.

And finally, Larry lets you view the process in action by providing evaluations to several of his consultation clients' stories. By having these writers identify the twelve story elements and essences within their own work, and then offering them his responses to their answers, we see first hand how the secrets revealed in *Story Fix* can lead storytellers to the *right* path for rewriting their novels and screenplays. Armed with the arsenal of weapons Larry offers in this book, you will not only fix your story, you will transform it.

And in the process, you will also be transformed as a writer.

—**MICHAEL HAUGE** (www.StoryMastery.com), author of *Writing Screenplays That Sell* and *Selling Your Story in 60 Seconds: The Guaranteed Way to Get Your Screenplay or Novel Read*

INTRODUCTION

This is a book about the writer within.

That sounds pretentious, I'll grant you. As if this book aspires to change lives and save souls.

Maybe it does.

Because, as writers, aren't we always seeking some combination of those two literary ambitions, either for our readers or for ourselves? Even if our most obvious intention is simply to entertain, we want our work to be remembered. When it is rejected, or even when we just know—in our heart or our gut, which in this instance is the same informant—we haven't nailed the story despite our best efforts, we feel as if our hopes have been dashed on the rocks of cold reality. We are all, at some point in our writing journey, well acquainted with that feeling.

This book is about harnessing that energy and spinning it into gold by seizing the inherent opportunity that awaits us in the *revision* of our work. When we approach revision with the idea of creating something more enlightened and empowered, rather than just making the writing itself technically better, truly wonderful things can happen.

Conversely, if we don't learn anything from our failures, or don't fully understand their nature and how we arrived at them, then we are trapped in a paradox of our own creation. That paradox is a crowded room, full of rejected writers who don't have a clue about how or why they failed in the first place.

Too often those writers will brush it off as bad timing, bad luck, or a lack of fairness. But almost always, rejection goes deeper than any of these reasons.

While we may not fully control the perception of our work, we are in complete control of how we internalize and apply the available knowledge from which we create it. Successful revision requires ascension of the learning curve relative to craft, finding and applying a higher level of knowledge in combination with any specific story feedback that fuels the climb. Sometimes we must revise without feedback, specific or otherwise, based on generalized responses or, once again, our own sneaking suspicions.

When a story succeeds, it is almost always indebted to some form and interpretation of knowledge—the conscious awareness of the elements that make a story *work*. When a story doesn't succeed, it is often because the writer is ignorant of those elements. Or, worse, defiant. This is true even when the writer stumbles onto a lucky streak but actually *knows* very little.

Which does happen, by the way. One of the reasons learning to write great stories is so challenging is that there are sparkling exceptions to every truism and principle that folks like me throw onto the craft pile. Not everyone who wins the writing lottery—meaning those few-and-far-between, best-selling, newly famous authors—can explain how they got there. Which means we can learn very little from them. Sometimes we guess, sometimes we just follow our gut or our heart, and sometimes that works. That said, writing a great story *isn't* a lottery. Much more is involved than a random collision of instinct and blind luck. Thus, strategy and knowledge can and should be a part of what we bring to the writing table.

Write from your heart if you wish. But that will get you nowhere, and slowly, if your heart doesn't know what it's doing.

The heart may desire, but the heart also needs to *know*.

Another reason successful storytelling is so difficult to grasp is that gurus on the subject spin writing craft in so many different ways. The collective conventional wisdom may smack of contradiction, when in fact it merely lacks clarity, or, just as often, simply stops short of considering the context of a bigger picture. For example, *intuition*—trumpeted by many as the key to the writing kingdom—is always an essential part of the creative process (in both the planning and execution stages of a story), but if you leave it at that, the odds of actually publishing your book successfully go down considerably. The real goal is to cultivate and *grow* both the breadth and level of your intuition—what I call your *story sensibility*—to the point where you can truly claim it as the source of your success. Luck will ultimately have very little to do with it.

Once you truly possess a keen sense of story, you'll notice that it embraces the elements of craft that may have been lost on you earlier. They actually become the stuff of instinct rather than an alternative to the nuts and bolts of craft.

Consider these common guru mantras, all of them real and attached to a familiar name in the story-coaching game: *Character is everything. Story trumps structure. Structure rules all. Plot is optional. Plot begets character. Three-act structure. Four-act structure. No-act structure. Core competencies. Realms of story physics. Snowflakes. Story planning. Story pantsing. Butt-in-chair, just write, go with the flow.* You can find workshops of all sizes, shapes, and styles, some even from actual authors of successful novels. That all of these approaches *do* touch upon truth and wisdom can be confounding.

When someone suggests following your gut by allowing what I call your *story sensibility* to lead into and through your story arc, that process is either valid *for you* or it isn't (which is different, many times, than being *right* for you, or not). It isn't a question of right or wrong, because the process is already wrong for some writers who create their stories in a different way. Writing by the seat of your pants is not valid for *every* writer; it's only valid advice for those who already have an informed story *sensibility* working for them. If you don't, though, and you nonetheless do as these well-intended mentors suggest—just follow your story instinct, allow the story and your characters to lead *you*—then this becomes the worst writing advice possible.

This dynamic is true in reverse. Story planning is not for everyone, because not everyone is capable of doing it either successfully or pleasurably.

It comes down to this: The exact same criteria, benchmarks, and the measurable and variable story essences that comprise an effective story apply equally to those writers who use story planning and those who don't. Nobody gets a free pass on the criteria for the creation of a good story. The path we choose is always heading toward that goal.

This is actually terrific news. Because it means, no matter what your favorite writing guru advises, that you get to decide which camp you belong to. As a storytelling coach, my files are full of clients who believed their story sensibilities were keen and evolved, and then after years and even decades of getting nowhere, they finally submitted to the guiding light of a given set of storytelling principles, which are nothing more than the proven, vetted instincts of an evolved story sensibility. Suddenly the clouds parted, and they finally got it. Suddenly all of those instincts have a name ... and its name is *craft*.

When revision becomes your next and perhaps only remaining option, you will benefit greatly from understanding how you may have cherry-picked through that massive bucket of conventional wisdom without actually distilling it into a *truth*—your own truth—that ignites and empowers the entire storytelling proposition.

You get to choose what knowledge you apply to your writing process. And your writing lives or dies by those choices. In the end, luck and instinct have very little to do with it, because both are expressions of what you truly understand—or don't—about storytelling. When that knowledge works for you, it's called *instinct*. When it doesn't, it's too often called bad luck in a tough business based solely on perception.

Certainly nobody knows everything there is to know about writing great stories. One of the most respected modern masters of this craft, William Goldman, assured us of this when he said, "Nobody knows anything." We can strive to *know* our craft, but we also have to listen to our inner storyteller and hope it has something good to say.

Sometimes we even get it right.

THE POWER OF INSTINCT

The power of pounding away at a story, driven by your instincts until it is forged into something precious, is not to be underestimated, but neither is it something you can count on. Relying on your gut or your heart only works when instinct is informed rather than blind. Otherwise it is similar to believing you can build a bridge because you've been driving across bridges for years. The writing guru who tells you that instinct is the only real means of writing a story and advises you to avoid anything that smacks of structure and craft might as well suggest that you go ahead and build that bridge based on your instincts alone, without any knowledge of the physics involved. Sometimes that works, but more often than not, in the hands of a newer writer especially, that splash you hear is the sound of the bridge collapsing under its own weight.

Story doesn't supercede structure: Story *is* structure.

Many famous authors, speaking in interviews that seek to illuminate their process, claim to have no idea where their story is going. What they fail to say, though, is that—based on the principles of craft—they do understand where the story *should* go, relative to the flow of dramatic structure and character arc. This partial picture of process suggests that you should (as opposed to *might*) just write, just trust your gut, and let the story tell you what it needs. For the folks in the workshop audience, many of whom are sucking up this guidance like Holy Writ, this is also among the worst writing advice ever given.

What these authors are talking about is their *process*. Don't be fooled into thinking they are advising you to chuck all the available principles of fiction and just wing it. They know those principles as well as they know how to boil water without consulting a manual.

Given that you're reading a book about fixing your story, odds are you are already aware of this well-intentioned sleight of hand.

It's always better to *know*.

Salvation—in the form of your next draft—awaits in a side-by-side comparison of what you understand about the craft, juxtaposed against how and where your failed draft (or simply an unpolished, less-than-final draft) came up short. In this context, the fix isn't merely a rewrite but rather, in a majority of instances, a re*thinking* of your story.

Knowledge swirls around us, waiting to be discovered.

Knowledge is like water, the stuff of life itself. It doesn't care what you call it, and it doesn't care if you recognize it; it's simply *there*. Consequences ensue when you take liberties with it, like diving too deep or long or failing to take in enough of it. It can even kill you if your instincts are off.

And so, to begin a quest for the rescue, resurrection, and redemption of our stories, we must first look within: at what we know and don't know, at what we're guessing, and at what we're missing altogether. Knowledge is there, where the seeds of our literary discontent have been sowed. Through its power, the fundamental tenets of storytelling craft, and a clean slate of opportunity, await.

This book is as much about rebuilding you as a writer as it is about rebuilding your story. You'll come to realize these goals are one and the same. We'll explore the mind-set required to successfully navigate the story-fixing waters, followed by the hard-core issues of craft that will empower that process toward effectiveness. Then, because a more ethereal discussion falls on deaf ears when the listener is less than fully enlightened, we will return to the philosophical truths about successful story fixing, using those tools and criteria of craft as context.

We don't just need to know how to win the battle; we also need to know why we are fighting the war. Such is the flow of this book: survival, warfare, and then the post-traumatic reality of encountering it all. Once we are introduced to certain principles, the entire discussion looks different on the second pass.

We don't send our soldiers into battle fresh out of the recruiter's office, no matter how badass they are. First we break them down through boot camp, run them through skill-specific training, and then rebuild them into warriors. It's the same for your story. You must confront who you are as a writer so you can be free to go to the next level in your writing journey.

There are no enemies in this battle, other than your unwillingness to embrace craft at its highest level. When you do so, everybody wins.

Nobody expects you to nail your story in one draft. But if the conceptual narrative idea is strong enough and your level of craft is deep enough, you just might get there in two.

PART ONE

THE RAW GRIST OF STORY FIXING

The blank page is perfect.
Not a single mistake to be found.
Anything that goes wrong from there has your name on it.

WHAT YOU NEED TO KNOW ABOUT STORY FIXING BEFORE YOU REVISE

As someone who has evaluated more than six hundred stories in the past three years, I've come to a certain realization I've not seen proclaimed elsewhere: Often the writing or the mechanics of a story aren't necessarily what bring it down; rather, it is the focus of the story itself, its level of inherent dramatic tension, thematic weight, and good old-fashioned compelling appeal that renders it unpublishable.

This is so obvious that it may not rock your writing world at first glance, but it should. Because, based on results, very few of those six hundred writers get that nuance. They simply chose the wrong story, or an inadequate story, to write. Their instincts didn't show them a higher bar to reach for, and their submitted stories bore evidence of that fact.

Chances are that nobody told you that your story was weak. Even with stellar writing and textbook execution, the story you chose just wasn't strong enough. Nobody at the writing conference will tell you this, or will even give you benchmarks or guidelines for determining whether your story idea is strong enough. This leaves you alone in determining how your story stacks up to the competition.

And that's the problem. At least half the stories I've read as a story coach—and, I'd wager, half the manuscripts rejected by publishers—are less about the writer and the execution than about the inherent appeal and strength of the story itself.

Writing *publishable* fiction, however you publish it, is a lofty goal when viewed from a qualitative perspective. Sure, you can publish anything you want these days, without vetting it (though rigorous editorial vetting is still the staple of traditional publishing venues and nearly any agent worth her smelling salts). I sometimes get nailed for saying this bluntly, but some writing groups favor a kumbaya approach to writing, in which any story is worthy and any writer can make it if he really, really tries.

This absolutely cannot be true. Not every story idea is worth pursuing, even in the skilled hands of the world's finest authors, and not every story written by a well-intentioned, even skilled, writer should be published.

I'm not seeking to discourage. I have no agenda in that direction. On the contrary, I seek to illuminate a realistic and achievable path toward helping solid writers create publishable stories, with a focus on turning pieces that aren't currently working into ones that are. And, as a bonus morsel of truth, all this stuff applies with equal validity and power to both rejected and newly conceived projects as well.

If you've been rejected after your best and highest effort, then you already know how challenging writing a great story, a publishable story, really is. I'm hoping you're ready to do the hard work—the real work and the proven work—that will take your story to the next level.

For the record, I agree with the kumbaya-humming groups about the part on trying. But it's the definition of what *trying* really means that's up for debate. This book is my take on that issue, with solid principles, logic, and proven experience to back me up.

TWO MAJOR REASONS WHY A STORY DOESN'T WORK

I believe that there are two major reasons why a story doesn't work, or doesn't work well enough, which in the realm of professional storytelling is the same thing as failing. These two categories are the very things a writer should strive to conquer, not just in the revision phase but from the story's inception.

If there are two reasons for why a story doesn't work, it follows that there are two reasons why it *does*, and that the first set is the antithesis of the latter set. Like an airplane must have both power and lift, an athlete must have both timing and speed, and a song must have both melody and lyrics to achieve their purposes, effective stories need two separate dimensions of energy.

Just two.

Either (1) your *story* proposition isn't strong enough, or (2) its *execution* isn't effective enough. The flip side, then, says that when a story *does* work, it is because the story proposition *is* strong enough and its execution *is* indeed effective. In either case, two coins are spinning in the air, and how they land determines the fate of your story. Mining the gold of this truth requires that you understand what *strong* means and what *effective* entails. Not everyone agrees, so whom you listen to becomes a factor in your success.

While this seems simplistic at a glance, the fine print attached to either area of weakness is not. There is a long list of criteria and common missteps within both of these categories, and because both are products of imagination and choice on the part of the writer (which are nothing other than your story sensibilities calling the shots), the remedy becomes as imprecise as the explanation of the problem.

Stories are like beauty.

Beauty is a perception, and perception is everything in certain fields of endeavor, including writing. The criteria for the *beauty* of both levels of story effectiveness vary widely and reside very much in the mind, if not the eye, of the beholder. In other words, one reader's masterpiece is another's waste of time and money.

This is why stories are usually rejected by one or more agents or publishers before finding a home. You'd think professionals would be on the same page about what works and what doesn't, but that's hardly the case. The eyes of those beholders have different tastes and personal preferences (which become *their* favored criteria) and thus different lenses through which they view a story. Writers are the first to determine (and are quite alone in doing so) what is beautiful and functional within their stories, and when agents and editors and readers don't agree—we've all heard tales of famous authors being rejected by dozens of agents—writers can always fall back on their hubris, reassuring themselves that those agents, editors, and readers *just don't get it.*

But your readers may very well have gotten it. They just didn't *like* it.

If you're in this business to actually *sell* your fiction, hubris will destroy you. Because those agents, editors, and readers *have to get it*. And if they don't, then it's on you to understand why not rather than, as a reflex or an uninformed response, attempting to breathe life into something that others perceive as comatose or flat or just less than compelling. It's up to *you* to realize that you aren't necessarily the arbiter of what is worthy and what is not.

You get a rejection, so in your state of denial you then decide to send it out to someone else. Not always the best approach. Then again, it may be the best choice available. You get to make that choice, and you have only your story sensibilities to guide you.

After a while, as more and more rejections pile up, we must consider the possibility that, at its core, the problem is with the *author* rather than those who have read and rejected the work.

You can revise anything.

It is always a question of degree, and sometimes *revision* is just another word for starting over.

If a story's weakness resides in *both* the story-strength realm and the craft-execution realm, then revision becomes nothing short of a complete reboot on multiple levels. In turn, this says something about the state of the writer's story sensibilities—the sum of instinct, knowledge, and experience, completely eradicated of ego—and becomes the first place to look for cause and effect as the revision process begins.

Story strength and craft execution provide an overarching context for the entire revision conversation. Determining in which of those two neighborhoods your work awaits is the first step in the revision process.

You have to decide. Which means, in order to do so with true confidence of your success, you have to *know*.

But how *can* we know?

Or better put ... *what* should we know, specifically?

There's a good—if not scientifically precise—answer to that: The perception (and thus the fate) of a story is in its measurement across several standards, which include simple opinion and personal taste. We have a proven set of principles, criteria, and outcomes to use as benchmarks to help us decide. You'll see lists of those in both realms soon enough, but for now, a higher-level view of story definition and storytelling craft is required.

We first need to tear into this story strength vs. craft execution issue and make sure our story sensibilities aren't out there on a thin limb, very much alone.

STORY AND EXECUTION

Revision isn't always a black-and-white proposition. In fact it rarely is. The two realms of revision—story and execution—are *not* mutually exclusive, but more often than not they act in tandem to sabotage the writer's best intentions. They remain separate in the sense that you need completely different literary sensibilities to master them. Conversely—and inevitably—if you come up short in either realm, the whole story will be perceived as highly rejectable.

A quick analogy might help you understand this. Two students try out for the college tennis team. This is Division 1, a high level of tennis by any standard. Everyone at the tryout can beat anyone at the country club, including the club pro. Here, at the aspiring-professional level, greater-than-average talent and instinct are required. One player is well trained but weak and sluggish. Her strokes are pretty, but her shots are cream puffs in a game that often depends on spin and velocity. Good enough for high school, but not for the tryout. The other player demonstrates great natural speed and racquet control; she can hit the crap out of the ball but makes bad choices under pressure. She lacks an evolved sense of judgment or patience to go for winning shots, and her double faults and unforced ground stroke errors are too frequent. Experience counts, and the lack of it can get you cut from the team.

In this case, *neither* player makes the team. The first player is told that her game is good but not great, not strong enough to compete. She's not quick enough, can't cover the court well enough, and her serve comes in fat, ripe for the opponent to rip a winning return. The raw material of her game isn't up to the level of the competition. Her game is generic. Other players who tried out brought a better game overall.

In this analogy, she is like the writer lacking in the story realm. This writer can write, but *what* she is writing is problematic. It's just too weak, and too generic; it doesn't stand out in a field of tough competition.

The other player, the one with the natural gifts, is told she needs to play the game at a higher level. She's a big hitter, but her instincts and timing are off. She'll get killed by a more schooled player, even if that player isn't as strong. It doesn't matter how hard you hit the ball if the opponent simply waits for you to get out of position to deliver a winning shot you can't reach. Everyone hits big at this level (which is why the first player was cut), and a sense of touch and anticipation is required to compete.

In this analogy, she is like the writer lacking in the execution realm. This writer's story rambles and includes side trips and diversions and lacks a sense of flow and structure. She makes bad choices at bad times, which is why in her career she consistently loses to authors with less raw talent.

Many of the other kids fail to make the team because they lack in both areas—they have a solid game but no differentiating abilities or skills, or a big game with no subtleties or touch. The two players described above define the scope of the specific improvements that might be required, and they fall into one of two realms: the raw strength and hunger that make a player powerful, or the timing and variable pace and patience that make a player formidable in all situations, at all levels.

Raw strength and athleticism (story) plus skill, timing, and intuitive sensibilities within the rules of the game (execution): The entire combination has to be stellar to make the team.

The rare player who brings this combination of talent to the tryout is like the writer who gets published. (And believe me when I say, when you submit a story to an agent or editor, you are very much trying out for a team, competing with other skilled writers against the same applied criteria.) If you display weakness in either the story or execution realms, you'll be like the rejected player walking home alone, bag in hand, wondering what went wrong and perhaps thinking, *They just don't get me.*

In fact, it is you who just isn't *getting it.* You showed up with only half of what you need to reach your goal, to compete at the next level.

The good news is that both areas of weakness can be strengthened, fortified, and fixed. But the writer needs to know where to focus the work of fixing her game in each area, because each requires the other. We need to bring the *whole* game to the tryout. If you continue to practice without changing your ability to achieve a higher level of play—and do the work necessary to execute it—nothing will change.

We need to know more about what causes stories to be effective in order to make it happen.

Once again, the two highest realms of story weakness are:

1. **POOR CONCEPTUAL BASIS OR STORY *IDEA*.** Your concept should lend itself to a dramatic premise and a thematic stage upon which your characters will show themselves. Without a strong initial idea, the story itself just won't be *compelling* enough at its core, no matter who is writing it. It may be too familiar. It may lack dramatic tension. It may feature a character who is flat and lacks a fresh edge. It may focus *too much* on character, without giving him or her something compelling to *do*. Or the story might simply be absurd, the leaps in credibility too vast. Revisions from this realm are challenging because you have to go deep into what you began with and change it. You can't tweak your way out of this problem. Revisions to these weak premises often fail because the writer attempts to polish the execution, when in fact the raw potential of the story itself—the inherent *nature* of the story—is not rich and compelling enough. It's like polishing a Volkswagen to prepare for a NASCAR race. Shiny isn't the point. Maybe *you* thought you had a great story idea, but based on results, nobody else agrees.

2. **POOR EXECUTION OF THE STORY.** The arc of your story's structure and the substance of its narrative are flawed. The story may indeed be conceptually strong enough, but the storytelling craft of the writer behind the wheel isn't. At least not yet. The writer isn't up to it, even if the original idea is. (See the case study in chapter sixteen for an example.) The narrative may be too slow, too laden with backstory, too one-dimensional. The character may be an archetype rather than an individual we are interested in taking the journey with. There is too little to root for, too little at stake. The

story changes lanes. The pacing is off. The list goes on. Maybe the story proposition really is on fire. But perhaps you and your current story sensibilities don't match up. Your story is bigger than you, relative to your ability to unspool the core narrative across an optimized dramatic arc. To nail *that*, you have to manage about eight dozen variables, which is like trying to juggle a ping-pong ball, a feather, and a bowling ball in a stiff wind.

Both weaknesses are fixable.

Nobody said this would be easy. It looks easy when you read a tightly written story, and that's the whole problem for many writers. It *looks* easy.

Here's a sobering and rarely spoken perspective: If 990 out of 1,000 manuscripts are rejected, why do we then believe that the percentage of acceptance will go *up* after revision when the same rejected writers are doing the revising?

Some stories will indeed be accepted after revision. Most won't. It is the *reason* that most won't that we need to embrace—and avoid.

Of those 990 rejected stories, about half will be dismissed because the story idea, concept, or premise just isn't good enough, even if the writing is perfectly fine. The other half will be tossed because the execution of a workable story just isn't good enough. And, in overlaying those two groups, a majority of the stories rejected will have issues in both realms. The rejection slip you receive, or the feedback given by a critique group or a beta reader, may or may not be clear about the underlying issues that led to this outcome. And few will actually go so far as to tell you that your story idea isn't strong enough, when in fact that may actually be the reason for its rejection.

To solve this paradox—that's what it is, and one of our own creation—we must dive deep into the reasons and origins behind the flaws that cause rejection in the first place. The more often rejection occurs—because the first response to rejection is usually to send the story to a different agent or publisher, sometimes that very day, without a thought about revision—the more valuable is this insight.

Story … or craft? Which realm of revision awaits you, and how can you know?

THE STORY-FIXING MIND-SET

Mistakes and weaknesses in our work, the stuff of revision and the raw grist of improvement, are almost always a product of the way we think colluding and colliding with what we believe to be true about writing stories.

Success, however, isn't necessarily a product of what a writer thinks and believes about writing. This is certainly not always the case for writers of bestsellers and breakout successes, or even for those who finally receive an acceptance letter after years of submitting their work. Often those joyous outcomes are the product of a revision process done well, applied to a powerful origin premise, all rendered by a capable writer and, lurking unnamed and underappreciated behind the scenes, a stellar story editor. But success stories don't always come with truisms and models, other than the observation that sometimes they cannot be explained. On occasion—and paradoxically, as this is the case with many breakout bestsellers from unknown names—success can be largely attributed to timing and pure luck, and less to artful craft and literary genius.

Need an example? Four words: *Fifty Shades of Grey*.

Even that story, as controversial and critically hounded as it is, must be recognized for its compelling *idea*. The novel and subsequent movie are pure strategy wearing the leather mask of creativity, tapping into a dark little corner of the psyche and speaking the unspeakable. Millions of women have flocked to it. Millions of men secretly hung on every word and were first in line on the movie's opening day. The strategic genius here, if not a shining example of literary art, is in grounding the story within a conceptual arena that has proven to be a sure thing.

Story execution—check. For better or worse, it was sufficient. But the story itself was brilliantly conceived from a *strategic* point of view, and that made all the difference.

THE VIRTUE OF AIMING HIGH

Welcome to the Crazy House of Writing Fiction, where anything can happen and where what does happen may not make complete sense. Either way, when lightning strikes or when darkness falls, it always has our name and the state of our craft hidden somewhere in the explanation.

One of the challenges I frequently sense in newer writers, or unpublished veterans, is that they don't shoot *high* enough or strategically enough at the story level. They aren't aspiring to greatness. Rather, they are seeking to write small stories, generic stories, with the goal of *somehow* making them great. Big difference there. They aren't seeking to blow the reader out of her chair with a story that hasn't been written before. It's as if they just want to see their name on a book cover, to simply join the midlist club, and they believe that piling on is the way to get it done. Another vampire story. Another dystopian tale. Yet another *Da Vinci Code* rip-off. One more love story straight off the assembly line at the romance factory. Another thrice-divorced detective with alcohol problems and a grouchy lieutenant. These writers seem to think they have to work up to a groundbreaking story by starting at a lower degree of difficulty, treading familiar turf, cutting their teeth on something less risky and compelling.

But if the goal is to get published and reach an audience, this mindset is exactly backwards. Stories from new authors land agents, get published, and earn market buzz precisely *because* they take chances and fearlessly plow new and provocative ground. The bookstore shelf is already full. Publishers aren't looking for mediocrity; they're looking for home runs. Gillian Flynn's mega-bestseller *Gone Girl* is a case in point. It's a character-driven thriller, and at a glance it contains nothing more conceptual than the rocky terrain of a middle-class marriage. But Flynn didn't settle—the novel is the antithesis of an American-dream slice-of-life story. Instead she delivered a deep dive into the darkest corner of domestic dysfunction, couching a highly thematic statement about the culture of media within a love story gone terribly wrong.

That story was *big*. It was huge. And what made it huge was the way she elevated the concept to infuse its premise with something we've never seen before.

Sometimes the risky bet is the best bet of all.

That effort begins, by the way, before a word of the manuscript has been written, at the *idea-concept-premise* stage of development. (If that's not the case, then you've just discovered a likely source of rejection and a subsequent need for revision.) In seeking to understand why your work has been rejected, this scope of ambition is a great place to begin looking.

What we write *in context to* informs the whole process of story development, and if there is no vision for the story and no box to put it into, then the writing can easily become a rambling search for meaning. Indeed, many early drafts are a search for the story rather than the execution of one. This single perspective explains why so much rejection and failure occurs among writers who don't yet understand what story development actually means.

To show how this looks in real life, at the end of this book I've assembled some case studies from my story-coaching work that demonstrate just how easy it is for a project to veer off the tracks at the level of concept and premise. What you'll read there shows the intentions of the writers—which too often reveal that they *intentionally* choose a story that is as stale as week-old bread or as full of holes as a block of Swiss cheese—followed by my analysis of how those intentions will play out in a manuscript.

Reading these *after* your indoctrination to the principles that make a story soar, and thus empower the story-fixing process itself, will greatly accelerate your ability to recognize your own level of understanding of the storytelling craft.

That level of understanding may not be what you think it is. If you start to sense this is true for you—if you are surprised by what you encounter—good things are likely to follow.

Here's a quick case study to tide you over.

This happened at a workshop for romance writers, who are among the most astute practitioners of craft in the business. Yet it is a genre full of writers depending almost entirely on their story sensibilities to get published.

I was lecturing about story concept, asserting that we must bring something conceptual to the story arena as the basis for a premise, something that is inherently compelling, and use it as the stage upon which the rest of the story presents itself. A story doesn't solely depend on skill and structure to work. The raw material of the story itself—the intrinsic, conceptual grist of it—is a huge factor.

A boring, normal, slice-of-life story told well will still be boring, unless that life is interesting … which by definition makes it conceptual. But a meaty conceptual framework—now that's something to work with.

So there I was, doing my whole concept-premise dance, giving examples, defining and comparing and contrasting, asking for the audience's concepts and analyzing them as a group. I'd just presented my favorite case study for concept: the vast oeuvre of the Superman franchise. Not exactly a romance, I'll grant you, but it's the poster child for the notion of concept as king.

That singular concept, the one that resides at the very center of the Superman franchise, has hatched ten films, hundreds of comic books, and two major television series. The lesson is this: Every single movie and comic and episode has its *own premise*. Ten movies, ten different premises. But each story is framed by—and arises from a landscape defined by—the central concept itself, which is the *same* for every story.

The conceptual notion is Superman in the *context* of being someone who is very different than the rest of us. That *difference* is the concept; it is what makes Superman unique and therefore fascinating. Not

Clark Kent the *character*, but his alter ego as the embodiment of something outside of what we consider normal. Without Superman, Clark Kent is inherently not all that conceptual. With him, though, the entire story landscape becomes astoundingly conceptual.

But notice, right here at the concept level, there is no *story* yet. You still need to add a premise—a villain and something specific for the hero to do, with something at stake—before this concept elevates to the level of *story*.

That seemed to work for my romance-writing listeners. Either that, or the principle wasn't yet clear enough to inspire pushback. We moved on to other issues with that principle in place.

On the second day, though, as we were diving into the writers' own stories and vetting them against all the requisite elements and criteria, one woman's hand shot into the air. I'd noticed her body language during the course of the workshop—squirming is telling, and facial tics speak volumes—so I knew what was coming.

Her voice was shaky, her tone challenging.

"I write romances. They're love stories about real people in the real world. I don't write about superheroes or murders or conspiracies or paranormal powers or schemes or whatever the hell you mean by something *conceptual*." She held up both hands and made sarcastic little quotation marks with her fingers. "So I don't really know what this has to do with me. Or with any of us."

If you've ever been in that moment, when someone calls you out in front of a group, when they have a legitimate point (one that was the result of my own failure to clarify colliding with her limiting beliefs that were squirming within a narrow paradigm), you know what that was like for me.

You could have heard a dangling participle drop in that room.

Romance stories present ripe opportunities for leveraging concept.

Leveraging concept within a romance is one of the best ways to elevate a story within a very crowded field.

But you have to dig for it. Falling in love isn't inherently conceptual, which means it's the writer's job to infuse the story with a conceptual proposition.

One of the writers in the room was enjoying huge success—as in, hundreds of thousands of copies sold in the past few months—with her latest romance, and I used that story as an example. The story (*One Lavender Ribbon* by Heather Burch, named by Amazon.com as one of the top one hundred best-selling e-books of 2014) had a killer concept, and it fit perfectly within what the group accepted as the confining conceptual tropes of the romance genre. And yet her concept—which didn't rely on superheroes or the paranormal in any way—was the context-establishing catalyst that made the novel work.

In her story a recently single woman buys an old house. As she begins to remodel it, she finds a stack of old letters hidden in the attic that tells a story—a love story—from half a century ago. Both the letters and the real-time story deal with war and tragedy, and evolve toward the mending of a broken heart as much as the discovery of new love.

Boom. There's a concept. No capes or ghosts or superpowers in sight—just some letters hidden for five decades in an attic. That's not a premise—it doesn't include characters or plot—but rather, it's a *concept*. And it's a good one.

The heroine in Burch's novel becomes fascinated by these letters. In seeking to heal herself, she decides to track down the author of the letters and return them to him (this is the premise—the letters become the catalyst that launches the heroine into action), and in doing so her path crosses not only with a handsome stranger, who happens to be the letter writer's adult son, but with an entire family dynamic that links to the letters and refreshes their recollection of war and their fear of loss.

This is a compelling fusion of concept and premise, with a heavy dose of theme as well. The concept stands alone before we meet anyone (because the house and the letters were there). It fuels the premise itself. It becomes the primary catalyst for the story.

The workshop ended well. The troubled writer now understood what I was talking about and later claimed it as a major epiphany. Her instincts had served her in the creation of a story arc, but the power of the story itself was the issue. Her instincts told her to avoid the conceptual, when in fact her approach should have been the opposite.

This is no doubt true for more than half of the stories rejected at the professional level. The writer is just fine as a creator of characters and scenes and sentences, but the *story*—the journey or quest you ask the hero to take—is unremarkable. Maybe even less than credible, possibly absurdly contrived. And thus, revision takes on a much deeper context than mere nips and tucks and tweaks, which are efforts to breathe life into the already terminally ill. Sometimes a better story, at the core level, is the best revision of all.

THE CHALLENGE OF EMBRACING GREATNESS

Writing stories can seem so simple, at least at a naïve glance, until one tries to do it in earnest. Many writers come to that first blank page after experiencing enrichment as readers, and they use that experience as the context for their version of how to write a story. It's no different than riding in the backseat of your family car as a child and then getting behind the wheel at age sixteen: Things are a little more complex when you're the one sitting in the driver's seat.

Often, lurking quietly in the back of these writers' heads is the smug sense that they can produce stories as good as those they read on a regular basis. This is a limiting belief—a delusion, actually—and the type of thing your inner writer sometimes needs to discard the hard way. Newer writers often bring a truckload of limiting beliefs to the process, many of them products of their experience as readers rather than their schooling as writers. We will try to dismantle them here.

We need to get schooled on the craft of writing to the extent that it trumps our untested instincts—before it schools us.

Boot camp is in session.

In any story, there is always something that could be stronger and more functional. In that sense the old writer's lament is true: Stories aren't ever really finished, just deemed sufficient. Or, in some cases, tossed into the marketplace, come what may.

To reach a truly adequate point of sufficiency, we need to examine the major pieces of the storytelling proposition from several angles. Overlap is inevitable—and valuable. After two decades of teaching this stuff at conferences and workshops, I can assure you that a significant percentage of writers don't "get it" the first time they encounter it and, if they truly want to move forward, they must immerse themselves in the discussion from several perspectives before an inevitable epiphany descends upon them.

Such an epiphany is an "angels choir" moment: The curtains part, and the writer finally grasps what she's been missing. The revision process then becomes a magical resurrection, taking the story and the writer to new heights that weren't even visible in the earlier draft.

The blank page at once calls to us and mocks us.
And so we fill it up with what we have to offer, arising from the pool of what we know, handicapped by what we don't know, and fueled by dreams we dare not utter aloud. Sometimes these intentions are soured by what we've chosen to ignore, or poisoned by things we have been taught that aren't true or applicable, either through ignorance or arrogance or simple haste.

Because, in spite of all the books and workshops and websites and analogy-loving writing gurus out there (I admit, I'm that guy), writers cling to the limiting belief that *there are no rules*. (That's semantics, by the way; the line separating rules and principles tends to blur.) The mere mention of that word—*rules*—causes us to rebel, perhaps even to conclude that *principles* and *standards* are really rules couched within softer verbiage. From there we decide we can write our stories any damn way we please.

Because this is *art*, damn it.

And *that* is a fatal mistake.

Professionals often do write their stories any damn way they please, and they do so because what pleases them is driven by those same principles that scare lesser writers away. The fact that they *know* what will make a story work, even before writing a single word, is the very hallmark of the word *professional* on their name tag. We must know what "doing it right" means before we can do it any damn way we please.

Often we don't discover that our work isn't strong enough until the rejection letter arrives. Or the critique group pounces like Fox News on the latest White House decision. Or the story coach doesn't tell you what you want to hear.

As part of the story-coaching guild, my job involves telling writers that their stories are coming up short, and why. Often I tell them that the wheels fell off at the conceptual starting gate. It's the *why* part that allows me to sleep at night, because I've been on the receiving end of the sharp pokes this business delivers plenty of times, and I know the value of *why*. Like a doctor giving a screaming kid a vaccination shot, I take solace in the hope that once the sting subsides the writer will see the pit into which he has blindly tumbled and will find his way out of it.

The thing is, you can't write your way *out* of the pit unless you know your story's weaknesses and how to strengthen and repair them. Such a statement creates a paradox of sorts, because if you knew what was wrong and how to fix it before you started writing, you wouldn't have written it with those weaknesses in the first place.

This is why revision is so critical.

For starters, we all do revision work, even before the book goes out to an agent or an editor. Even "polishing" is, in the truest sense, a form of revision, and as such we should subject it to the same rigorous standards that a criticized story must endure.

Revision assumes you now know what you didn't know before. It assumes you understand whether your rejection was the outcome of unaligned taste or bad market timing (which may not require revision), or due to a story that is broken at its core, or has been poorly executed (which absolutely does require revision). When you don't know the difference, your stories will continue to fail. And it won't just be the story's fault. It will be yours.

WHAT WENT WRONG

The entire notion of *fixing* your story manifests within several contexts. While they are slightly different goals, the unifying objective is nothing less than *rehabilitation*.

Like any rehab program, this book focuses on the core values, techniques, and proactivity that were lacking when the original version was written. These weaknesses in the initial draft resulted in the need for repair and upgrade. From this perspective, during the revision process we are examining the touchstones and goals that we should have established from the outset.

It's easy to just sit down and write something. It's just as easy to simply change something. In this way, writing and revising can be fun, addictive even. But like any addiction rehabilitation program, fiction rehab requires courage, honesty, transparency, vulnerability, support, guidance, and a vision for what is possible. And most of all, it challenges us to stay away from the toxic behaviors that put us in rehab in the first place.

Because writing a great story, one that works on all counts, is anything *but* easy.

ACKNOWLEDGMENT IS ALWAYS THE FIRST STEP

The addicted have no chance of recovery unless, and until, they claim their demons.

With failed manuscripts, we're talking about conceptual and narrative flaws. Misdirected approaches. The undervalued and ignored.

The unseized dramatic opportunity. An unenlightened process. As stated earlier, an agent or editor will rarely clarify any of this when he rejects you, and it might not even show up in the catalytic critique that brought you face to face with the revision phase.

Successful rehabilitation is never a simple, linear process. "Just put your butt in a chair and write" is as naïve a cure as "Just stop drinking, damn it."

If, for example, the story is deemed "too slow" or "nothing special, been there, read that," there may be several causal factors buried within that critique. It's like going to the doctor and saying, "I don't have enough energy lately." Your complaint could mean just about anything short of having fallen off a roof. Before the ailment can be diagnosed and the healing can proceed, we need more information, perspective, and principle-based modeling.

The goal of this chapter is to introduce you to tools that will help you begin to self-assess your novel, using any specific feedback you have received to point you toward possible suspects.

MAYBE YOU'RE ONE OF THE LUCKY ONES

Maybe you know precisely what needs improvement in your current novel or screenplay. Maybe you can account for why it was rejected or the target of someone's soul-crushing criticism, or even why the soft voice in your head keeps whispering that it's not yet good enough.

But you probably have no idea whatsoever, which puts you in the middle of a crowded demographic. You're mystified because your beta readers all loved your story.

Either way, in order to fix the thing, you'll need to target specific issues of a conceptual, structural, and narrative nature rather than simply polish the manuscript, which only works after you've plugged all the leaks.

If you only did the polish, hoping to hit the sweet spot of agents' and editors' expectations, then you'd be guessing. But guessing may have been what got you in this mess in the first place. You need a reliable process to fix what needs fixing.

To complicate matters, the criticism you receive about your story is often unhelpfully vague. It can sound like this: "The story is too slow. I never really liked your hero. I was confused. Nothing grabbed me. I lost interest. It's too familiar. It's bland and flat. You lost me in the second half. I didn't like the ending. We have something just like this on our list. It was too far out there; this could never happen, and I never bought it. You must have been high when you wrote this. I hate stories like this. It's too dark. It's not funny. The writing is too purple. It's too violent. Too sexual. Too on-the-nose. Too preachy."

Or the most useless and dreaded feedback of all: "I dunno—it just doesn't work for me."

All of these things may be true.

But how, then, do we fix our stories when we hear this kind of feedback? These are *perceptions*; they are qualitative, imprecise, and immeasurable. Like someone citing a "rough childhood" to explain a troubled life, these criticisms are vague ways to describe issues with one or multiple story elements and essences, perhaps rendered by the hand of a fellow writer in waiting. You may have underplayed some things, overplayed others, or completely ignored or fumbled some of what a story needs in order for it to work.

The good news is that there is a dependable starting point to get to the root causes of these and other perceived story weaknesses. The weak link may be hard to find, but it's always there, hidden among the interdependent chain of these twelve graded story competency issues. Success resides in knowing where to look for that weakness and, when you find it, how to connect the cause to the effect and upgrade accordingly.

But even that is problematic if you don't understand or accept what the story criteria and elements are, or what they even *mean*. Chances are nobody will tell you *that*.

Selling a story is an all-or-nothing proposition.

Publishers don't take on a "promising" story, and they aren't willing to help you bring it up to their standards. It's not like they're a college recruiting an up-and-coming scholar or athlete; they're looking for performers who are ready—right now—to step onto center stage. Your story has to *work*, completely and powerfully, without a hitch, in order to be published. Which means that one single weakness, even nestled among other stellar story elements and essences (the former being *what* you wrote; the latter referring to the contextually informed *meaning* of what you wrote), may take you out of the game altogether.

It's a scary prospect. But you need to be within spitting distance of *perfect* for the genre and reader niche you are targeting.

EVALUATING THE TWELVE SPECIFIC STORY ELEMENTS AND ESSENCES

Your challenge in this chapter is to grade yourself on each benchmark. Assign a grade based on what is currently on your pages, using the familiar scholastic report card grading scale, letters A through F. Writing isn't a pass-fail proposition, at least in this context. But it *is* a pass-fail proposition when you submit your work to an agent or a publisher; you either land the deal, or you don't. But at the *story-fixing* level, we will be dealing with increments of effectiveness, the sum of which results in that pass-fail outcome.

That outcome is a qualitative assessment, with infinite gradations between "It's great" and "It sucks." To get into this school—the Academy of Being Published—you'll need a GPA above 3.00, with no Ds or Fs in the bunch. A 3.50 is even better, but lesser novels get published all the time. If you've been rejected, it may not mean you are currently below a B average (3.00), but it may mean that one or two of your C grades are deal killers—like a great singer who can't hit the high notes—which can't be offset by an A in other categories.

In my book *Story Engineering*, I cautioned that all six of the core competencies of successful storytelling need to be executed at a professional level. Mastering five of them could result in a stellar story, but that one instance of mediocrity will get you rejected. This is the scary, rarely spoken truth of writing for publication (which includes self-publishing with the intent to gather a readership, as well as selling your screenplay). Essentially, and almost completely without exception, you have to nail all of it.

And even then, to break in, one or two of these story elements or essences need to be A-plus stellar. This home run mentality among publishers is complicated by the fact that established A-list authors actually can get away with writing stories devoid of glow-in-the-dark elements and essences. But don't be fooled, and don't be tempted to point to a novel by a familiar name to make this statement false. A-listers do have something stellar going for them, and it's often a home run—it's their *name*, their brand in the marketplace, which sells books even when the story isn't particularly fresh or powerful. Publishers value the name brand as much as the next great story idea. We are actually trying to break in to that exclusive club of A-list names, but the only way to do it is to be better than those famous authors by giving readers something brilliant.

Grade yourself as follows using these benchmarks:

- An **"A" (4 POINTS)** when the story element or essence in question is a fresh and compelling asset rather than a handicap. The element or essence should be something you'd find in a bestseller, something worthy of mention in a stellar review.
- A **"B" (3 POINTS)** when the story element or essence in question is fine but not particularly remarkable. You get to check it off as present and accounted for, but it's not what a critic would consider the strongest aspect of the story, and possibly she's seen it before.
- A **"C" (2 POINTS)** when you have to think hard about how your story meets this benchmark and you honestly realize that there's a chance nobody will notice or remember it. It's generic, vanilla, cliché, like the detective with a drinking problem. It's just *there*: not broken, but not remarkable either.
- A **"D" (1 POINT)** applies when you *think* the particular element or essence is there, but you're pretty sure it comes up short against the given benchmark criteria. It's just not doing what it is supposed to do for the story.

- An **"F" (0 POINTS)** when the element or essence in question is missing entirely.

Feel free to add a plus or a minus if you're stuck between grades (because sometimes you're just a tweak away from something special). The point is to know where you are so you can know where you need to go next with the revision.

Either way, you need to *know* where you stand, element by element and essence by essence, across all twelve story criteria.

The real value here is in the definitions and benchmarks shown for each individual element or essence. (These benchmarks can be found in the chapters in Part Two.) Often when a writer comes up short in any of these areas it's because she simply doesn't know enough about it, which you may soon realize.

For example, the most frequent story-level misstep is confusing *concept* and *premise*, which are *different* elements, though they are inextricably connected to the point where confusion is common. This one, in particular, can sink your story.

We need look no further than the bestseller lists to see this truth in action.

Bestsellers arrive in one of two categories: books by established A-list authors, and new authors with extraordinarily compelling novels. Notice that within this latter category, nearly every entry is a "high-concept" story (as opposed to a character-driven, trope-dependent premise), while those from established authors are more premise-driven, or at least the extension of a conceptual notion they've established in earlier works (Harry Potter, for example). Branded A-list writers like Nora Roberts don't always need a killer concept, because their name and talent can drive a concept-light premise into the end zone. But for the rest of us, a premise empowered by something highly conceptual—thus requiring that we understand the difference—is an immediate attention-getter, taking the place of the brand equity that established authors can leverage.

If you simply can't recognize what will compel agents, editors, and readers—because you are only applying your own opinion in this regard—then you are stuck in a paradox of your own creation. An evolved story sensibility is not just your opinion; it's something a professional will assess in considering what will work. And it is your story sensibility that allows you to distinguish between a high concept and a concept that is harder to isolate within a premise.

Think of it this way: Your novel is like a business, which means that what the customer wants is critical. It is the product; you are the proprietor. You may like mustard on your peanut butter sandwiches, but if you open a restaurant with this particular concept, you're gonna be upside down in no time. A massive percentage of rejected stories can be explained by the author writing what he *thought* was compelling— that's what all of us do, every time, relying on the keenness of our story sensibility to make the right choices—only to find himself on a tiny island of minority opinion in that particular regard. And there are very few potential customers on a tiny island.

Confused? Congratulations! Here is your first story-fixing opportunity.

To nail your novel you need to be crystal clear about the differences between *concept, premise, theme*, and *idea* (in addition to several dozen other points of craft), and how those will play in the commercial marketplace. And because these terms—*concept, premise, theme*, and *idea*—are merely labels given for completely independent yet requisite story elements, the vocabulary itself is rendered arbitrary. In the real world these terms are interchanged regularly among agents, editors, and especially reviewers, thus muddying the waters for writers attempting to navigate them. In Part Two of this book, you will receive definitions that will serve you in the quiet of your own writing space. You should also check out the case studies offered in Part Four to see how this misunderstanding compromises a story at square one.

As you engage with the process, remember two things.

First, anything short of total honesty and vulnerability is cheating, and the loser in this shortcoming is you. You are looking for opportunities to improve your story, so don't give them away by refusing to see or acknowledge the problems others have perceived.

Second, you are revising because you already suspect—or perhaps flat-out know—that your story isn't working as well as you intended or as it should. This means you can't give yourself As and Bs across the board at this stage. Frankly, hardly any story out there, even the most lauded bestsellers by the most respected authors, will earn straight As for all twelve essential story elements and essences.

Know this: If you have a bunch of C grades, or lower, among your twelve—or even *one*, for that matter—your novel or screenplay is probably not salable if you're an unpublished writer. Works by previously signed writers get editorial input and a second chance, but new submissions do not. The goal is to assess and elevate your story to a B or better for all twelve criteria, so put your most sincere effort into honestly pegging where you are now.

While this may feel like an earth-shattering experience, at the end of the process you will have a game plan that perhaps didn't exist before, one that will empower your story-fixing efforts toward greater effectiveness. This is the means of finding out what you don't know, what you fumbled, what you weren't told in that rejection e-mail, or what simply wasn't such a good idea after all.

So let's get started. Let the story fixing begin.

THE VALUE OF KNOWING WHERE YOU STAND

You may soon realize that the biggest benefit of this process is discovering you have a D on your hands for a given story element or essence. Because now you are no longer kidding yourself or working blindly. This is an opportunity to bring something better to your pages.

At that point you'll be given the chance to use the listed definitions and criteria in Part Two to develop an alternative narrative approach for that element or essence. This will put you on a path toward improving your story, repairing and strengthening it. At the same time you will be improving *yourself* as a writer. You'll soon be someone who *gets it* rather than someone who guesses at it.

It is critical to understand that your grades aren't the point. Using your new awareness to strengthen the *story* is. Your grades will do absolutely nothing for you until you use them to make yourself a better storyteller.

Don't yield to the temptation to simply respin a rationalization of what you have. No one will ever see that rationalization except you. Rather, use your revised story element or essence, created in context to your now-higher understanding, to raise the bar for the revision itself. In doing so you are beginning the revision process here and now, grade by grade.

As you proceed through this book and delve deeper into your revision, applying keener perception and expansion of these principles, you may want to return to this chapter. I recommend you use a separate page to log your grades and the revisions made in response to them, because you might find yourself running out of room. You may even find yourself completely reinventing your primary story thread. These core competencies and realms of story physics combine and interact with each other to the extent that only when you have embraced them all will you be fully empowered and enthusiastic about your story in a more holistic and integrated way.

The Grades

So here we go. Grade yourself on each of these twelve elements and essences, A through F, based on what you know and believe *now*. Later you will be asked to grade your answers again based on an elevated understanding and revision of each element or essence, as empowered by the definitions, criteria, benchmarks, examples, and discussion you will have internalized.

If you aren't entirely sure of what some of these terms mean, that's fine for now, although this lack of knowledge just might be the root of the problem. You will thoroughly understand them soon enough. Just grade yourself to the best of your current understanding.

STORY ELEMENT OR ESSENCE	GRADE (A–F)
1. Concept (the presence of something conceptual)	
2. Dramatic premise/arc (hero's quest, goal)	
3. Dramatic tension (conflict via antagonistic element)	
4. Vicarious reader experience	
5. Compelling characterization	
6. Reader empathy (what the reader roots for)	
7. Thematic weight, relevance, and resonance	
8. Effective story architecture (structure)	
9. Optimal pacing	
10. Scene execution	
11. Writing voice	
12. Narrative strategy	

Some writers may recognize these elements and essences. This list combines what I call the *six core competencies* and the *six realms of story physics*, grouped by their natural affinities. A powerful premise, for example, leverages the existence of dramatic tension via an antagonist-driven conflict and is contextually influenced by concept. Characterization, as another example, is measured by the degree to which readers engage and empathize with—root for—your hero along the path you've created for her.

The core competencies are the essential building blocks of a story (elements), while story physics are the relative forces (essences) with which the core competencies are applied to achieve the highest level of reader involvement and emotional investment. One is the machine; the other is the fuel.

Like spices stirred into a simmering pot of your favorite recipe, these story ingredients meld into each other to become a sum in excess of their parts, inseparable and dependent. The cook must be in command of both realms—the spices brought to the kitchen and how they are mixed, as well as the method of cooking—before the dish can become delicious and memorable.

Including one less-than-fresh ingredient or getting the proportions wrong results in a meal that disappoints. Our stories can be scrutinized in a similar way.

How did you do?

It's not impossible, or unexpected, to find that you've given yourself all As and Bs. And yet, someone out there doesn't agree. Make no mistake: You *need* the agreement of agents and editors (and in the case of self-published authors, critics and readers). This is a fact that can put you in a confusing situation. To move forward, you must open yourself to the possibility that you aren't yet in command of these story elements and essences, and/or the art of combining them within the context of the narrative flow of your story.

This is the most common dilemma of all. A writer thinks her story idea is terrific. The agent or editor doesn't agree. Who is right, and who is wrong? That's less important than who has the power and who doesn't at the moment of submission.

What follows in Part Two is a solution to this dilemma. For each of these twelve story issues, you'll find definitions, criteria, discussions, and examples that will allow you to develop a higher level of understanding, one that may lead you to a higher grade and hopefully toward an evolved or simply stronger set of creative choices that will result in a stronger, more compelling story.

That will get you into the storytelling game at a professional level. But to break in, to really deliver the goods in a competitive market, you'll need more than twelve definitions and their corresponding criteria. You'll need an evolved *story sensibility*—what some might think of as *talent*—that leads you toward a seamless and powerful exposition within the framework of your story. The goal isn't to land on what *you* think is a great idea; it's to understand what the readership you are targeting will be drawn to.

Be patient with this growth process.

These tools cover the gamut of what you need to know in a technical sense, and they'll ultimately lead you, over time, toward a higher level of artful narrative execution. The degree to which you own these principles, the more you use these tools and recognize them within stories you read, the sooner you'll reach the point of commanding them yourself.

Remember, in effect you just took a pretest. You're invited to come back to these twelve elements and essences to grade yourself again after you've immersed yourself in the expansion, discussion, and criteria-based clarification of each, which is the stuff of the remainder of this book.

Don't lose sight of the goal. We are working toward a *professional* level of storytelling. Story *selection*, apart from your story*telling* (execution) skills, is half the battle. When your story comes up dry relative to these twelve criteria—either before or after you've submitted it—pay close attention. That's your evolved story sensibility telling you that this piece may not be strong enough at its core.

Maybe a revision will do the trick.

PART **TWO**
REPAIR

"Knowledge is power."

—FRANCIS BACON, 1597

"What you don't know can kill you."

—MURDER, SHE WROTE, 1996

4

STRENGTHEN YOUR CONCEPT

This is where the story-fixing process gets fun. It is also where it gets tricky. Far too many new writers begin the storytelling journey without an awareness that one of the most deadly pitfalls of all awaits them at square one of the process ... which is the development of a compelling story *concept*.

WHAT IS CONCEPT?

In the context of story repair, concept is one of the most likely places to find weakness, so it is the natural starting point for strengthening your story. Unfortunately, concept is also the most overlooked source of failure in a sea of rejected manuscripts.

Concept is like a battery for the story itself, imparting energy and life to whatever is connected to it. And the last thing we want is for our stories to run out of juice before the finish line.

Before we dive in ...

The first few chapters of this book divided the reasons behind rejection into two categories, story and execution. Both realms for revision bear reiterating because we're about to rip into the first one.

- **STORY ISSUES:** The big-picture proposition of the story isn't strong enough, the story doesn't grab or compel the reader, or it's been done to death and there's nothing new or fresh. (This is covered in chapters four through six.) "Story" can be defined as the combination of concept and premise. Weakness occurs when the premise isn't infused with something that is intriguingly conceptual in nature, meaning there is nothing within the story that creates an arena or a compelling foundation upon which to build.

- **EXECUTION ISSUES:** Your execution of the premise across the entire arc of the story doesn't deliver as promised. Something is off among the core competencies (often because of the story's structure, or lack thereof) and available story physics, which are the forces that create reader empathy and response. (This is covered in chapters seven and eight.)

A weak concept can be strengthened and saved.

Almost always, the source of weakness and dysfunction within a story dwells in the nature of the concept itself; i.e., the degree, or complete lack, of something *compelling* within the concept. It's hard to turn a boring concept into a compelling premise, and yet, this is the golden ring of revision. We need to do precisely that, usually by adding a conceptual layer rather than by looking to the premise to fix the problem.

The good news is that you can apply a dependable list of criteria to a story concept for benchmarks that open up different avenues for creating a more compelling story execution. The bad news is that weakness in any one of those criteria can cripple it.

With these criteria in front of you, you can elevate your concept from "Meh" to "Oh my!" with a little understanding and creative thought. Letting go of what you have, as tough as it can be, allows out-of-the-box thinking to drive the improvement effort. This renders recognition of weakness as the first step in the repair process, because that recognition allows you to jettison the weakness and replace it with something better. Out-of-the-box thinking is often more productive when there's a specific target to aim for.

Fair warning, though: Concept is a tricky issue.

Concept confuses many at first glance. The result of that confusion explains half or more of the rejection slips written over any given time period as agents or editors judge the story idea to be simply too dull.

The source of writer confusion is that any and all story ideas already have a concept, by default, which makes developing that basic concept a *qualitative* challenge.

For example, you could write a novel from this concept: "a story about a guy living alone in a big city." That actually *is* a concept, just not a very compelling one, which becomes even more obvious when you measure it against the given criteria. At first there's nothing interesting or unique about the protagonist, the setting, or the situation. It's flat, and therefore dead on arrival. You don't need to chuck it, but you do need to *enhance* it to save it. Good concepts go beyond the banal to offer something fresh and, most of all, compelling, and this example is nothing if not generic and bland.

A better concept might look like this: "a story about a wealthy widower who suddenly finds himself alone after thirty years of marriage and moves to Los Angeles to live with his younger brother, a film director who enjoys life in the fast lane. The man must negotiate his staid values and comfort level with the onslaught of aggressive, sophisticated women who seem to want to rescue him from his depression." I don't know about you, but to me that sounds like a significantly more compelling story than the first concept. If you don't agree, then the issue resides with your story sensibility, which is the key variable for what you decide to write. We live and die by what we decide in this regard, so the key is to look outward, at the readership, rather than inward at what we are drawn to personally. I encounter this particular concept issue frequently with my coaching clients, and often their response to my feedback is something like, "Well, I intended that. It's obvious that something else will be in play that complicates his situation."

It's *not* obvious. Never assume an agent, editor, or reader will expand the scope of your concept in his mind because it's obvious to you. If the juice of your concept is layered, define the layering at square one.

The second example meets several of the criteria for a compelling concept, one of which is this: The reader hasn't encountered this story before, or if she has, this offers a new and intriguing twist.

The acid test of a compelling concept is simple.

If you pitch your concept—without having to add elements of the premise to make it interesting—and your listener responds, "Wow, now *that* is interesting. I can't wait to read a story based on *that* idea," then you've hit pay dirt. If you received that response, then your concept is, by definition, compelling and intriguing, at least to that particular listener. The trick is to offer something that a stadium full of listeners would respond to in the same way. When it happens, the concept has already fueled the ensuing premise—*any* ensuing premise that leverages it—with compelling energy.

As you are about to learn, a great concept could connect to many possible premises. This notion, too, is one of the criteria that, when applied, will ensure your concept is on fire.

The word *compelling*, however, is a mixed bag.

Reaching for the bar labeled *compelling* presents an opportunity to add depth and richness to your concept. Yet, "compelling" always remains a matter of opinion. What is compelling to some may be considered trite and ridiculous to others. That's why we have different genres. Readers of romances may not find the notion of traveling to a different dimension to encounter an alien life force all that compelling. Even if it's a romance, if you set it in an alternate universe, then it is also something *else*.

There are no hard and fast guidelines for attaining a "compelling" level of appeal. One agent's next *Hunger Games* is another's been-there-read-that story. For the writer sitting alone in his office, this leaves little to work with other than his instincts. This is why one of the recurring themes of this book is the development of a cutting-edge, highly market-accurate *story sensibility*, because without a commercial nose for what masses of readers will find appealing, a writer's notion of "compelling" may fall short.

The goal of all of this, at its highest level, is to evolve your story sensibility.

You want to be able to look at your existing story concept and say, "Yeah, that's good. It meets all the criteria," or admit, "Well, I thought this was cool, and it *is* cool for me, but I can see now how others might not agree, because the story is nothing special. It's thin on drama and vicarious experience, and my premise has too little to work with."

As I've said before, you may like mustard on your peanut butter sandwiches. But good luck trying to launch a chain of sandwich shops based on that concept.

Elevating your story sensibilities becomes the most potent tool of all in the revision of a story. With concept, an idiosyncratic story sensibility shows itself immediately, via the criteria and then via reader reaction to the idea itself. Thus a concept can either make or break your story before you write a word.

For the purposes of this discussion—indeed, as context for the entire fiction-writing proposition—think of the word *concept* as an *adjective*: that which is *conceptual*. The real question about your story idea becomes "What is *conceptual* about the story idea?" even before you add a character or a plot (which, upon doing so, places you in the realm of *premise*, a related but different story element).

Here are some examples of inherently conceptual concepts.

These concepts meet the criteria for a compelling concept without delving into premise. Notice how there are no heroes here, no plots, no actual story. Each of these is an *idea* for a story that has been imbued with a *conceptual* layer, which renders it immediately compelling, at least to the market sensibilities of the people you are trying to impress. It may not be your thing, which means you shouldn't write that story … just as you shouldn't write it if your story sense tells you that you alone hold affection for it. Some of these have been taken from best-selling stories you might recognize, while some are concepts that promised a story the writer(s) couldn't quite deliver on.

"Snakes on a plane" (a proposition)

"The world will end in three days." (a situation)

"Two morticians fall in love." (an arena)

"What if you could go back in time and reinvent your life?" (a proposition)

"What if the world's largest spiritual belief system is based on a lie, one that its largest church has been protecting for two thousand years?" (a speculative proposition)

"What if a child is sent to Earth from another planet, is raised by human parents, and grows up with extraordinary superpowers?" (a proposition)

"What if a jealous lover returned from the dead to prevent his surviving lover from moving on with her life?" (a situation)

"What if a fourteen-year-old murder victim narrates the story of her killing and the ensuing investigation from heaven?" (a narrative proposition)

"What if a paranormally gifted child is sent to a secret school for children just like him?" (a paranormal proposition)

"A story set in Germany as the wall falls" (a historical landscape)

"A story set in the deep South in the sixties, focusing on racial tensions and norms" (a cultural arena)

CONCEPT DEFINED

The best definition of concept, because it is a multifaceted proposition, resides in melding *all* of the following perspectives, resulting in one conceptual identity:

- Concept is the central *idea* from which a story emerges.
- Concept is an arena, a landscape, a stage upon which a story will unfold.
- Concept can be a proposition, a notion, a situation, or a condition.

- Concept can create an alternate universe or setting with its own physics, dangers, and challenges.
- Concept can be a time or a place, a culture or a speculative imagining.
- What makes an idea a *concept* is the presence of something conceptual.

In general, if you can add "hijinks ensue" to the end of your concept, you may be on to something good. If the hijinks themselves lend a conceptual essence to the idea, then include them in your statement of concept.

Keep these examples front and center as you engage with the definition of, and criteria for, the form and function of *concept*, which is the delivery of a *conceptual* layer to a story idea. When in doubt, return to these examples as models of concepts that work, not only because they meet all the criteria (which you are about to be given) but because they are simply rich and fertile soil from which to plant and grow a killer story.

THE CRITERIA FOR CONCEPT

The definition for concept has the criteria itself embedded within it. To help you wrap your head around this, here are those criteria lifted and listed as actionable, gradable benchmarks and relational elements.

As a consistent measure, a good concept is inherently interesting, fascinating, provocative, challenging, intriguing, disturbing, engaging, even terrifying, before adding character or plot. When this is a majority opinion, especially within a defined genre readership, then you have the basis of a successful story.

High Concepts vs. Real-World Concepts

High concepts depart from the norm. They exist at the extreme edge of imagination and possibility. High concepts are simply more *conceptual* than more common, real-world concepts. (Real-world concepts, too, can be rendered conceptual at their core through expansion via premise. This means that if you're pitching and you don't include that conceptual layer in your pitch, you're leaving ammunition on the table.) Examples of high concepts would be Superman and Harry Potter and the Avengers, which bring in fantastical and supernatural elements. Examples of reality-constrained concepts that are equally compelling would be James Bond or Alex Cross or *The Help* or *Gone Girl*.

Stories about real people in real situations also benefit from something that creates a compelling context for the story. Something about a hero can be conceptual, or something a character does or believes or must deal with can be conceptual. For example, one of the main characters in *Gone Girl* conspires to kill herself while framing her husband for her death; this becomes the concept itself.

Concepts, high or otherwise …

- can be character-centric, like the above examples.
- can be a speculative proposition, like *The Da Vinci Code* or *Star Wars*.
- can be thematically conceptual, like *The Help* or *The Cider House Rules*.
- can be lifted from perspectives and drama in the real world, like a story about the 1980 U.S. Hockey Team or *Apollo 11*.
- offer a setting, time, or place rendered conceptual by virtue of the promise it makes: The forthcoming story will play out there. Historical novels live and breathe by this conceptual potential.
- could be about stories set within a given culture, such as *Fifty Shades of Grey* or a story about The Blue Angels or even The Hells Angels.

Notice how all of these examples are different than—more conceptual than—a "story about a guy living alone in a big city." Nothing about that particular concept is unique or fresh. It doesn't push buttons; it doesn't appeal to a given demographic, interest, or fascination; it doesn't pose an intriguing (at least, intriguing enough) speculative question or proposition; and it doesn't unfold within a setting, time, or culture that would allow the reader to take an appealing, vicarious trip into such a place.

Great concepts always promise a vicarious ride for the reader. They can take readers somewhere or place them into situations that are not possible, realistic, or even something they would choose in real life. A strong concept takes readers on a ride of a lifetime, one they will never know in their personal reality.

A concept can define the story world itself, creating its rules and boundaries and physics, thus becoming a story *landscape*. (Example: A story set on the moon is conceptual in its own right.)

A concept can inject speculative, surreal possibilities, such as time travel, ghosts, paranormal abilities, cloning, etc., into an otherwise normal reality.

In short, a concept is simply the *compelling contextual heart* of the premise and story built from it. It imbues the story atmosphere with a *given* presence. It elicits that sought-after response: "Wow, I've never seen *that* before, at least treated in that way. I really want to read the story that deals with these things."

It does *not* include a hero ... unless the hero is, by definition, a conceptual creation, which is the case in several of the examples just given. A story is built around a protagonist leveraging her conceptual nature. The character isn't the concept—because every story has a protagonist or hero. What makes her fascinating, and therefore conceptual, is the proposition that renders her unique and appealingly different (think Nancy Drew, Stephanie Plum, or Wonder Woman). When that difference screams for a story to be told, you have a great concept on your hands.

It might be helpful to consider what another story *without* a vivid concept would sound like in a pitch: *Two people fall in love after their divorce.* It's not a bad story if you can pull it off. But divorce is all too familiar and therefore not a strong concept by itself. An agent wouldn't quickly invite you to send him a draft; he'd want more from the concept, leading into a premise that picks up the conceptual power it offers. If you could bring something contextually fresh to it—for instance, *Two people who both want to murder their ex-spouses fall in love*—then the story is already strengthened from its conceptual promise alone.

Agents and editors are looking for something fresh and new—in other words, they are looking for the *conceptual*. When a concept is familiar and proven—which is often the case in romance and mystery genres especially—then fresh and new becomes the job of premise and character, as well as voice and narrative strategy. Imagine, for instance, that you are an agent and this pitch crosses your desk: "My story is about a detective who is assigned to find the killer of a girl." This common concept crosses my desk regularly, and my feedback is easy: "There's nothing here that sets your story apart. You've defined the genre itself without adding anything inherently appealing." You might as well have said, "My story is a by-the-book detective mystery."

No sale.

Also, here's a cautionary tip for self-published writers. When I say, "Agents and editors are looking for something fresh and new," it may be tempting to say, "Well, I'm not dealing with them. I'm going directly to readers, so I don't have to worry about all this fresh concept stuff." That's risky thinking. Readers screen titles online, looking for pitches—concepts and premises—that draw them in. It's the exact same dynamic, with the exact same risks (concepts that are too flat and familiar) and opportunities (concepts that make readers think, *Now that sounds interesting*). As a self-published writer, don't make the mistake of thinking that you have different story criteria, that the bar is somehow lower for you. If you want to succeed and build a readership, the exact opposite is true. You are still competing with the biggest names in the business, and frankly you are at a disadvantage in pursuing self-publishing, so your story needs to be exceptionally strong at both the conceptual and premise levels.

Concept is genre driven.

Literary fiction and some romance novels and mysteries aren't necessarily driven by concept. However, the subgenres of romance—paranormal, historical, time travel, erotica, etc.—are totally concept dependent. Other genres, such as fantasy, science fiction, and historical fiction, are entirely driven by and dependent on concept.

If your concept is weak or too familiar within these genres, you have already substantially handicapped your story.

The purpose—the only purpose—of concept is to give your premise something to work with, something that fuels that story world, the characters, and the situational dynamics with conceptual givens, suppositions, truths, and constraints that drive and color everything that happens. When those aspects are as appealing as the concept itself, concept and premise as a team become a whole that exceeds the sum of each part. They become the stuff of bestsellers, the ignition of careers.

Given that dynamic and the dependent relationship between concept and premise, it behooves us to understand the highest definition of premise, which is almost always less intuitively obvious and accessible to newer writers based on instinct alone. Too often they are writing about an *idea* or a *theme* rather than a dramatic arc driven by a fleshed-out protagonist's quest.

While concept serves as the framework for the story, the premise is the substance of what *happens* in the story, and to whom, for inherently interesting reasons. When you break that definition down into its parts, you find another set of purpose-driven goals and criteria for premise that help clarify how it is indeed different than the concept from which it was culled.

We further define premise and explore its criteria in chapters five and six. We're pounding on concept here, because concept is the prerequisite for a premise that holds promise. Make sure you have internalized concept before moving on, and that you dive into the next two chapters with an informed context for the discovery of the amazing potential of a well-executed premise.

For now, let's go back to your story's concept and rebuild it ... the right way.

WHAT IS YOUR CONCEPT?

Having just been exposed to the highest definition and criteria for excellence in concept, write down the concept for your story now. Make sure you don't go into the realm of premise to do it. Focus on the core idea, cull its conceptual essence, and state it in context to the story arena, proposition, landscape, or framework you are putting into play as the basis for your premise.

Is this a new take for you? Perhaps you've already discovered a lack of conceptual essence in your story, or, even better, you're already working on enhancing your concept.

It's also possible that you're underwhelmed. Concept can seem so obvious, so preliminary, that some writers—newer ones in particular—discount it in their eagerness to dive into the premise itself. But that's like stepping over a dollar to pick up a dime, because your premise may only be worth ten cents if you fail to infuse it with compelling energy via a glow-in-the-dark concept.

Concept is the most undervalued, most underserved, and potentially most powerful of all the available story elements. It trumps character and your narrative skill in virtually every commercial genre, with the possible exception of *literary* fiction (where it is nonetheless valuable, just not the reader's highest priority, and thus, not the writer's focus). As stated in the last chapter, when a new writer pens a bestseller, or even when a new writer breaks into the business, the story almost always possesses a compelling concept that creates context for that author's stellar execution.

The flip side can be true as well, and perhaps it's true for you: As I've said—actually, as I've *warned*—a huge percentage of rejection is connected to a weak or too-familiar conceptual context for the story.

How did you do?

Is your new concept better already? If so, celebrate, because what happens next—a new and higher execution of premise—may be the most joyous writing experience of your life. An explosion of potential may dawn before your eyes. If your concept meets the criteria and is, from your most advanced and enlightened story sensibility, something that will draw in readers, then perhaps your story-fixing issues reside elsewhere. Keep your strong concept in mind as we delve into those deep waters in the ensuing chapters, because sometimes a great concept gets lost in the complexities of story execution.

Remember that the issue isn't whether your story *has* a concept or not (if it has characters in it, it does) but rather how compelling, fresh, edgy, provocative, and flat-out interesting that concept is. Again, it is a *qualitative* proposition, one in which you are looking for greatness rather than a placeholder.

Concepts are to stories as people are to personalities: Every person has a personality, for better or worse, but some individuals are so flat-lined that we say they don't have a personality. Ironically, people with *toxic* personalities (you know who they are) *are* conceptual because you can spin stories about them, so this isn't a question of positive or negative. Big, bad, dark concepts are often rich and promising. Rather—for both this analogy and for your stories—it's a matter of presence versus absence.

Here's an analogy. You always supply a résumé when you apply for a job. If the page is blank, then you still have a résumé ... but it's one that won't work. The lack of a résumé is, indeed, still a résumé—it says a lot about you—but it will fail to get you the job 100 percent of the time. The same is true for your story's concept. Maybe you haven't given it a single thought. Maybe you don't think you have one, or worse, you don't think you need one. In that case, your concept is simply this: *The story is about someone or something, without any complications or opportunities that create intrigue and interest.* Period. This isn't good enough.

Does a romance novel have a concept? Does a mystery have a concept? Does a historical novel have a concept?

Within these genres, the respective genre tropes *become* part of the concept. They are integral to the concept, and they speak volumes about the context of the story. Your job is to take that generic concept higher, with something specific and conceptual layered onto it.

Genre tropes are nothing short of reader *expectations.* Two people meet, they fall in love, it isn't easy, they deal with it, they end up together ... yeah, that's a concept. That's a *romance.* Someone commits a murder, an investigator gets involved, clues and complications pop up, and the perp is finally identified. That's a concept. That's a *mystery.* A tale unfolds amidst a specific historical time and place we are familiar with. That's a concept. That's a *historical* novel.

And yet, standout genre stories bring something more conceptual that extends beyond those genre expectations (tropes), something unique that frames the story within those expectations, all inside the parameters of the definition and criteria for concept. Thus those concepts, and the stories built from them, stand head and shoulders above the hoards of rejected manuscripts that didn't take it to the next level.

Imagine *2001: A Space Odyssey* without HAL, the ambitious computer with human qualities. HAL was the concept: *What if a computer took control of a mission based on its own agenda?* The story wouldn't be an iconic classic without that concept. It would be just another lost-in-space story, undistinguished and forgotten. The genre itself— science fiction, a spaceship lost in space—is fine, but it was made so much stronger by the addition of a rogue artificial intelligence computer taking over. From there the premise was already on steroids, ready to give readers something they'd never seen before.

The *story*—the plot and the character's quest—emerges via the *premise.* (We dive deeper into premise in chapters five and six.)

EXAMPLES FROM STORIES YOU KNOW

For the most part, the iconic and celebrated series novels of our times are born of a killer concept. A series is defined by its concept, even when each installment has a unique premise. In fact, each installment does have a different premise—a unique plot dynamic, with its own obstacles, stakes, and resolution—that arises from a singular concept, the one that defines the series itself.

Harry Potter is a character, but he is conceptual: He has wizardly powers, and he attends a school for emerging witches and wizards. That's the concept, right there: "Harry is a young wizard, and he attends a prep school for fledgling wizards and witches." There are no stories yet, no murdered parents, no bullies and villains … just this concept. Everything that happens springs from it.

This single conceptual notion exists across the entirety of the Harry Potter series. The series brings in other congruent elements, such as the macro premise (Harry finds and brings justice to Voldemort, who killed his parents), but each book or film has its own plot (premise), rogues' gallery of villains, and stakes.

Make sure you wrap your head around this point—it's the *same* concept throughout every book or film across the entire series. Many rejected series proposals and manuscripts get shot down because the overarching concept is weak (it doesn't meet the criteria), creating a challenge for each installment to stand alone within that same thin contextual proposition.

Every superhero story you can think of is based on a fresh, highly compelling concept. The heroic essence—not the humanity of the character—*is* the concept. Batman is a concept. Superman is a concept. RocketMan, Wonder Woman, Stephanie Plum, Sherlock Holmes, Jack Ryan, Harry Bosch, John Corey, Jack Reacher, and Holden Caulfield … all are heroes and heroines, and all are conceptual in nature. We read those stories for the hero, as much or more than we do for their premises. That's concept trumping premise, which is the secret weapon of creating a great series. The concept is everything.

But concept, especially in stand-alone novels, isn't the sole province of heroes and villains (character). Many things can be rendered conceptual and can thus create a context for plot. Examples include a magical ring that has the power to enslave the world, the opposing factions in a fantasy based on the War of the Roses, the existence of a covert "Impossible Missions" force, vampires falling in love with human teenagers, a dead girl narrating from heaven, a talking teddy bear who is still alive and talking when his owner is grown, a ghost avenging his own death, a story set in the raging heart of America's bleakest racial tensions, and a marriage so dark a woman is willing to die to frame her husband for her murder.

These are all *conceptual* and come from best-selling novels and/or hit films. Standing alone, without premises, they aren't stories. However, each is already set up to be compelling because of its concept, which contributes rich dramatic fodder to the story that arises from it.

The prime-time television series *Castle* is a stellar example of concept versus premise and resides within the particularly challenging detective mystery genre. The show applies a different dramatic *premise* each week but always maintains its *conceptual core*: Rick Castle is a novelist and friend of New York City's mayor. The mayor authorizes him to shadow real detectives on cases to do research for his work, and he ends up contributing his crime-solving acumen to each week's caper. Castle is a character, but it is his conceptual nature and the conceptual proposition of the show that become the concept of this program, which never varies from week to week. The premise, however, does differ from week to week, because each episode has its own plot.

Nearly every film Tom Cruise makes is highly conceptual. It seems to be the primary criteria for the projects he takes on. A man who dies over and over again, only to return to face the same problems (*Edge of Tomorrow*). A guy living on a desolate planet, serving as its repairman (*Oblivion*). A jet jockey with an attitude (*Top Gun*). A hustler with an autistic brother (*Rain Man*). A pool-playing prodigy (*The Color of Money*). A guy who gets shot up in Vietnam (*Born on the Fourth of July*). A German officer who betrays Hitler (*Valkyrie*). The list goes on in this conceptual fashion. Notice how the arenas—aircraft carriers, war, the handicapped, post-war life, outer space—offer a conceptual appeal, as much or more than the characters themselves. This is the power of concept at work.

Every novel Jodi Picoult writes is based on a conceptual centerpiece. Elephant researchers. Medical life extension. The social culture of wolves. Columbine. Her stories are, in effect, cultural and even historical studies in the form of a novel, and all are conceptual by definition because the culture or the history attracts us before we meet the protagonist or sense the plot. Which is rendered, by the way, not like a documentary but according to the criteria of a dramatically driven premise.

These aren't slice-of-life stories. Those have a place on the shelf, but not within commercial genres. If you've tried to write your genre story—romance, mystery, science fiction, fantasy, western, historical, paranormal, war story, and so on—without installing a conceptual engine to propel it forward, that could explain your rejection in a nutshell.

Think of any blockbuster novel or film. The odds are almost certain that you'll find a conceptual idea or framework at its heart.

You can certainly, and quickly, find examples that seem to refute the notion that concept is the stuff of success: historical, episodic renderings of slavery and war, sagas about families settling the Wild West, and biographical stories of courage and genius. But notice that these are almost always either true stories or overtly literary undertakings. And even then, if you look hard enough you'll notice something conceptual at work. If nothing else, the appeal of the historical significance is conceptual in its own right, as in the films *Twelve Years a Slave* and *Selma,* or in any biopic of a famous historical figure.

LET THERE BE SUPERMAN

Of all the iconic characters in fiction, one stands out as the quintessential hero of both print and screen, the ultimate poster boy of *concept.* He wears blue tights and a cape, and he used to change out of his suit and into his costume in a telephone booth, in a time before cellphones. His name is Superman. And he has a lot to teach us about concept.

As I mentioned before, the character Superman *is* the concept. As one of the most conceptual characters of all, he is someone who embodies something conceptual that defines the context of the stories he appears in.

In a story about the spirit of a jilted lover haunting his old girlfriend, the ghost is the concept. Sure, the ghost is a character as well, but first he is a concept. When you throw in the notion that the ghost helps his girlfriend solve his murder—or, even better, that the ghost sets out to prove that his girlfriend perpetrated his murder—you've added a *premise.* This particular premise is, in fact, from the 1990 classic film *Ghost*, starring Patrick Swayze and Demi Moore.

Other examples in both classic and modern literature abound. In *The Great Gatsby*, Gatsby is the concept. He's a guy who sought to become rich to win the love of a girl. That's a concept.

We are looking for an *essence*—a quality or a power or a gift or a shortcoming—that is conceptual, that imbues the story with compelling energy, even before the character inhabiting that essence walks (or in Superman's case, flies) onto the page.

Faster than a speeding rejection slip ...

As of this writing, ten major Superman films have been released, in addition to hundreds of graphic novels. All of them have different premises, because all of them have different plots. Which leads to the accurate conclusion that premise *is* plot.

And yet, every single one of them leverages the *same* concept: *An alien infant is sent into space to escape a dying planet, crashes on Earth, is discovered by humans who raise him, and demonstrates superhuman powers as he grows into manhood.*

Remember the television program *Smallville*? The writers evolved that concept into a different story: *Let's look at the teen and young adult years of that alien boy.* That, too, is simply a concept, and a great one.[1]

Superman as a character meets all the criteria of a killer concept. Many different stories could arise from this concept, because it is fresh and different, it is rich with dramatic and thematic potential, it creates a wonderful story landscape and arena for the stories that arise from it, it has massive potential for conflict and confrontation with an antagonist (the villain), and, most important, it is simply and almost overwhelmingly compelling.

A concept does not ask a dramatic question, such as "Will Katniss survive the Hunger Games?" Unless the hero *is* the concept, which happens in stories with Superman and Batman and Michael Connelly's Harry Bosch, a character isn't even included in the concept statement. And if the character *is* the concept—at least within the statement of

---

[1] For the curious, the ten films featuring Superman can be found at www.supermanhomepage. com/movies.php.

concept—the focus is never on what *happens* to that character. What happens is the province of *premise*, which we put under the microscope in the next two chapters.

WHAT IS CONCEPTUAL ABOUT YOUR STORY?

What is the notion, proposition, situation, story world, setting, or fresh take that creates a framework or arena or landscape for your story, one that could hatch any number of stories, and one that doesn't require us to meet your hero or know your plot to make us say, "Yes! Write a story based on *that*, please"?

The world, and the publishers and readers who live in it, isn't going to get all that excited about another detective, another great romance, another ghost, another gun fight, or another medieval bloodfest unless it is somehow rendered fresh, new, and provocatively fascinating at its conceptual core. *Outlander*, for example, had time travel, which fused romance and science fiction within a medieval story landscape. If your concept is a commodity, make sure there's a unique twist involved that elevates it and keeps it out of the hands of the discount shelf crowd.

You are holding the secret weapon of storytelling in your hands. Think bigger. Go further. Make your concept more conceptual. Maybe your story's salvation is as simple as that.

Maybe that's why you're here, wondering where your best opportunity for fixing your story resides.

Maybe, though, you now know what went wrong, having shone a light on your weak concept or the absence of something conceptual within your story. Maybe, now that you know, it's staring you right in the face.

Is your concept truly in line with the grade you gave it? Can you do better?

Feel free to grade your concept again by creating new versions of it until something conceptual resonates. Pitch your favorite to others, and see what they say. (Even if they don't understand the difference between concept and premise, you'll be listening and evaluating with an informed ear.)

What is your concept? What is conceptual about your story?

Developing a better answer to these questions might be the impetus you need to get it back in front of an agent or a publisher.

The Flip Side: Concept as Deal Killer

Then again, maybe your concept is just fine. Maybe the problem—the weakness—is in your premise, or your execution of it. Those issues are next. But they are irrelevant if the concept that fuels them isn't meeting the available criteria. It's like sending a soldier into battle without everything he needs to protect himself … he'll get taken out early. Concept is like that. A great concept is your best defense against rejection.

Concept touches everything within a story. It colors, imbues, ignites, and affects each and every story beat. This means you can't just toss in a conceptual idea up front and then pay it no mind as you begin to tell the story. With a stronger concept comes a stronger premise in response, and you are the author of that level as well. It won't happen on autopilot, but it will be there for you to work with when your concept has been elevated. But you have to follow through.

Take your concept to a higher level, and your story is already a step ahead of the many others in the agent's in-box. You now have a live wire to power the story that follows.

And you might have just salvaged your story.

5

EMPOWER YOUR PREMISE

At some point in the process of selling your novel or screenplay, you will be called upon to pitch it. Agents, acquisition editors, and film executives receive pitches almost daily and thus are prone to a natural cynicism and impatience because so many pitches are less than stellar—and many are downright awful. These gatekeepers absolutely *want* to hear a great story pitch, and when they do, their enthusiasm will be obvious. You'll get a green light to submit more material down the line, on that story or another one.

The biggest mistake of pitching is when the writer launches into a sequential *synopsis*, without an overview that includes a concept, a premise (including a character/hero intro), and perhaps a theme. A pitch can take many forms, but the most basic is a one-sentence summary that touches on several key story elements: the conceptual basis of the story, the hero, what the hero needs and wants based on a problem or opportunity, what opposes the hero's quest, and the stakes.

There's a word for all of that. It's *premise*. A *synopsis*, or even an *outline*, is nothing other than an expansion of a premise.

Premise is the most important element in the entire realm of story development. It *is* the story in preview format. Everything you seek when you are building the story is pulled from it. Screw it up, and the story suffers. Screw it up badly enough—by leaving out key elements—and the story bombs.

You need to get the premise right. And it begins with understanding what a solid premise is, what it covers, and why those elements need to be there.

When an agent or editor passes on your story pitch, it's because the premise is, in her eyes, lacking in some way. Even if your concept grabs her, your premise might tank the story if it's not strong. The rejection could be due to factors other than a weakness in the story—it might be too close to something she's currently working on or something already in the market; it might be too derivative or too dark, etc.—but most of the time it's because the key elements of the story and the critical realms of story physics are simply not present, or at least not working.

Let me clarify one thing before we fully define *premise*. I mentioned that a good pitch begins with concept. It certainly does. But concept remains distinct and separate from the story's premise. Be clear on that. In the last chapter we looked at concept from all possible angles, sometimes juxtaposing it against premise. In this chapter, beginning with the forthcoming definition of premise, concept is not included. And yet, a good premise is imbued with compelling energy because of the concept from which it sprang. Keep that straight as you engage with this chapter, because mastering both concept and premise becomes a sum far in excess of either part.

PREMISE DEFINED

If concept is the foundational proposition—the stage—of a story, then premise is the drama you set upon that stage. Premise is, in essence, the plot itself, driven by the character's or hero's decisions and action, summarized in one or two sentences. It describes a hero's quest or mission that stems from a newly presented or evolved problem or opportunity and is motivated by stakes and consequences. Finally, there is a villain (or other antagonist, which doesn't have to be human or even a living thing; it could be weather or disease, for example) blocking the hero's path, creating confrontation and conflict that requires the hero to take action to achieve resolution.

THE GOAL OF PREMISE

Like concept, the highest purpose of your premise is to *compel*, to create the linear framework for a dramatic story that gives your character something interesting and emotionally resonant to do. If you land on a bland, familiar, slice-of-life premise, you can still pitch it by covering these bases. But like a soup made of just water, salt, and a few beans, it won't draw crowds.

Concept, on the other hand, creates an opportunity for a more compelling story to emerge. In that context, concept is a tool, a catalyst that is applied *to* your premise, something that underpins it.

Pop Quiz

Based on the definition and discussion above, what is the premise of your story? Write it down using only a few sentences. If you need a true synopsis to cover the given criteria, consider that you haven't clarified the core story yet. If it takes more than a few sentences to convey, the story may be too complex for its own good. And *that* may be the source of the rejection that brought you here.

Now consider this: How does your current premise align with the following criteria?

- Your premise introduces a hero, with a glimpse at how and why we will find this character or this arena interesting (that is, *conceptual*). If she isn't all that interesting, then your premise is already suspect.
- Your premise delivers a snapshot of the hero's journey within your story. Your hero has a problem or an opportunity that calls for a response in the face of opposition to the goal. Something is at stake. If the premise is simply to *observe* a character's life (which is a common story killer), or to episodically show us who he is throughout a journey with no stakes-dependent goal or specific mission, then it is suspect.
- The nature of the hero's journey is *dramatic*. Conflict is in play, forcing the hero into confrontation. Obstacles create and define

that confrontation and conflict. The quest or journey challenges the hero and draws out her courage and cleverness, which become instrumental in reaching the goal of the story, and thus the resolution. The pursuit of the goal takes the hero into uncharted territory—both internally and relative to what opposes her—by forcing her to confront inner demons in order to square off with the threatening exterior opposition. If the *only* antagonist in the story is an inner demon, your story may lack dramatic tension and stakes. Inner demons are a complication to the confrontations with villains rather than the antagonists in their own right. Conflict is the lifeblood of fiction, and it needs to be readily visible in your premise statement.

- The premise gives the hero something to *do* in the story. And because there are stakes attached that resonate and elicit reader empathy, we are moved to root for the hero along the path of the story quest. If we have little or nothing to root for—if situational observation is the only narrative grist—then the premise is weak. Your hero needs an external foe to banish.

- The premise should align with the tropes and expectations of its genre. While a genre story can be character driven, it must have a conceptual context that aligns with the genre, forcing the hero to take action against an external antagonistic force rather than simply existing as a situation within the story world while we watch the hero observing and responding to what is going on around him.

- The premise should give us something new and fresh. Even if the genre defines familiar territory, give readers an original take on it. The highest goal of premise is to seduce, to make people want to read the story. In that sense, premise leverages the underlying power of concept to become bigger and better than before.

If you sense an overlap between the criteria for concept and premise, you are correct. But it is necessary to understand how they are the same in terms of objectives, and how they are different in terms of specific elements and essences.

Premise: Good, Better, Best

Any premise is better than no premise (which happens, especially in slice-of-life stories that lack a true dramatic plot or an antagonistic element), but, as with a concept, simply having one may not be enough. It is a matter of degree. Some premises are stronger than others even when they share a concept. The difference is the strength of the *drama* a premise promises, as opposed to just the intrigue of a static situation.

A story about two guys robbing a bank has strong possibilities. But it's a lousy pitch if left to a simple logline, even if the writer has more in mind than this simplistic setup states. A story about identical twins robbing a bank owned by their father is a better story. But the best story would be about identical twins robbing their father's bank because someone has kidnapped one of their children, and the only means of coming up with the ransom is to convince their father to give them the bank's money, even though he is facing an IRS audit and a past-due Mafia loan. This is the best premise of the three because it is more detailed; the dramatic tension, conflict, and stakes are clearer and play at a higher level; and it is working with a deeper concept.

Never bet your premise on an implication that more is going on than what has been stated. A love story about two people in a small town has potential, but if that's all there is—two people in love wandering around a small town—it's a poor premise. A love story about two people of different races in a small Southern town in 1965 is a better premise. An even better premise, though, might be a love story with even more going on: The lovers leverage a dirty little secret about the mayor to force him to call off the lynch mob that promises to disrupt their wedding. The FBI intervenes using a trumped-up charge at the behest of the mayor, whom the governor helped get elected because of their shared racial bias. Now we have a more layered story with deeper thematic chops and more urgent stakes.

Notice in these examples how the premise moves from good to better to best by adding two realms of story physics:

- a higher level of conflict
- a deeper empathy for the characters

Both are choices made by the author, available at any time during the story development process, including the revision stage. The more story physics you pack into your premise pitch, the better it will work, not only as a pitch but also as the basis for story development. Because the higher purpose of a premise is, in fact, to ground the story in the author's mind in a way that keeps the narrative on track rather than allowing the plot to ramble and drift.

THE BIG MISTAKES WITH PREMISE

Stories are often rejected at the premise stage, even before a single word has been read. Why? Because they lack a clear *promise* of drama, conflict, stakes, and emotional resonance. An agent, editor, or prospective reader needs to sense that those elements will exist, so it behooves writers to make them as obvious as possible within the premise.

Slice-of-life stories that primarily ask us to observe a character moving through a specific circumstance or story world, without a real quest and stakes that inspire empathy, and that depend on backstory and characterization rather than drama, immediately raise a red flag. Story is *conflict*, and if this conflict doesn't scream from the premise itself, it will be difficult to convince agents and editors that it will work at all. The real deal killer here is a writer who tries to create a literary story within the realm of genre fiction, which is like asking an audience to be interested in Hulk Hogan's high school transcripts instead of rooting for him to throw Dwayne "The Rock" Johnson into the cheap seats.

Another potentially poor, frequently off-point premise is the telling of the life story of a fictional character. Stories that encompass a famous person's entire life (or most of it) work because we're already interested—the protagonist is the concept in that case—but that same interest doesn't extend to a fictional hero. Your hero needs a *specific* problem to solve and/or an opportunity to go for. She needs to encounter specific obstacles that stem from external sources. Something needs to be at stake, and the story should follow a singular plot arc rather than a series of vignettes or anecdotal episodes. If your pitch includes the words "the adventures of," which is as episodic as it gets, the odds of acceptance and success go down considerably.

Episodic is a bad word when pitching a premise, and toxic when it is an intentional goal of story planning. Two people who travel to Southeast Asia and have adventures is a weak premise. There isn't a plot, and other than a few microdramas, no dramatic tension is involved. We may like these characters, but the story doesn't give us much to *root* for. It's a diary, and a diary is not a novel an agent or editor will want to see.

Some writers push back on this, citing books like *Eat, Pray, Love*. Sure, it was a bestseller and a hit movie, and it didn't have a plot. It was, by intention, episodic as hell. But *Eat, Pray, Love* is *not a novel*. It's a memoir. If you're writing fiction, you need a plot—no exceptions. Even stating your intention to make your story "character driven" will send agents and editors scurrying into a dark corner of the writing conference in hopes of avoiding you altogether. The only avenue for a plotless, episodic, character-driven, slice-of-life novel, no matter how beautifully written, is in the literary genre, which is among the most difficult genres to crack. If your story comes anywhere near this description, you may have just found your explanation for rejection and a game plan for revision.

Even if your story *is* literary, an agent will ask you to provide more than your protagonist's backstory and angst. You'll need to tell an in-the-moment story, one that showcases all the character facets you hold near and dear and positions them as catalysts, obstacles, and complications with an external hero's quest. In other words, a premise.

If you are writing fiction, your story needs a plot. It needs a dramatic premise. The more original and compelling, the better.

EXAMPLES OF PREMISE

Let's look at a couple of bestsellers to showcase their concepts and the premises that flow from them, each culled and described separately.

Nelson DeMille's bestseller *Wild Fire* has a killer concept: High-ranking patriotic political zealots perpetrate a heinous act of terrorism on their own country (the United States), rationalizing the loss of lives as the cost of a noble goal. They then seek to place the blame on Middle East extremists in order to motivate a massive military response that will take out the real terrorists once and for all (in other words, make the president angry enough to strike back). Because of the buttons this concept pushes (which I call *narrative strategy*, one of the six realms of story physics), we are already on board. In fact we're rooting for a hero to stop these psychopaths before more American lives are lost.

All of that is the *concept*.

The *premise* is the story of a former military intelligence officer who is sent in to solve a crime that is later revealed to be connected to this plot. He must overcome a cover-up among high-level players who are in on the scheme before he can expose their diabolical plan and bring them down. All of this plays out while a time bomb that would most certainly incite the next world war ticks in the background. That's a massively dramatic premise with huge stakes that readers will engage with on an emotional level and that may even inspire sympathy for the patriotic villains, as well as the protagonist.

In Gillian Flynn's *Gone Girl*, the concept is that a wife could, if so moved, disappear and fabricate incriminating evidence that makes her death appear to be a murder committed by her husband. This is a juicy concept that taps into the heart of the emotional fragility of marriage and the desperate means that someone sufficiently resentful and hopeless might resort to for revenge.

The *premise* shows us this entire process with the introduction of the wife and husband in context to the history of their relationship, which has become cold and toxic. The appeal is twofold: First, we are privy to the moment when Amy, the "missing" wife, confesses her machinations, which will cause her husband to be indicted for murder. Second, we watch as the two players outsmart each other with Machiavellian tactics, each move unfolding with the seriousness of a chess match. This causes the wife to make even more diabolical plans behind the scenes, completely and totally humiliating and subordinating her husband with threats he cannot comprehend. Both players win and get what they want in a compromised form (the husband gets to be with his child, and the wife gets the husband), but they must sink to new lows of deception, extortion, and sacrifice to maintain a level of fraudulent compatibility.

The result is brilliantly told, and the author amply rewarded: *Gone Girl* was a runaway bestseller and an Oscar-nominated film. At the heart of that success was the concept itself—it fueled the premise with can't-look-away darkness that delivered a wickedly delightful and vicarious experience for the reader/viewer.

Certainly Flynn didn't settle for the first story idea—concept or premise—that came to mind. She set her bar high and demanded an extraordinarily powerful set of story physics from both.

That opportunity also awaits you, as you seek ways to fix, elevate, and resurrect your novel prior to reintroducing it to the marketplace.

REVISE YOUR PREMISE

Using these proven criteria for effective premise, juxtaposed with the grade you assigned yourself for the premise you wrote down, and in context to your newly empowered understanding of the relationship between concept and premise, take another swing at it. Give your premise even more punch with a highly visible potential for dramatic tension and reader empathy. Using one or two sentences, make us want to read this story.

Do any of your grades improve with this new, stronger premise? They just might, if your prior awareness and feel for the power of premise was lacking, even a little.

THE COMPLICATION OF PREMISE

Here's the challenge about premise: What may appeal to you may not resonate with agents, editors, or readers. Just as with concept, only your story sensibility determines how close you come to commercial viability. This cuts to the core of whether a story will soar or remain a niche tale that appeals to only a small reader demographic.

This is art, too. You get to choose. Are you writing what *you* want, or are you writing to build your career as an author, which requires you to be strategic and clever in your story choice? Choose carefully, and then adjust your dreams accordingly. They don't call most writers starving artists for nothing. And regardless of your choice, the craft side of the proposition remains the same: There are tools that can help you achieve what you seek to attain. Only the choice of scope and the proportions of your concept, along with the premise that flows from it, determine the difference between big and small, between art and commercial appeal, in this regard.

Writing for yourself, to heal or speak your truth, is a noble endeavor. But it may not get you the success you hope for. Writing for others, for commercial gain only, can be an equally dark path, leaving your story without emotion or artistic merit. The best strategy of all is to do both. This is why you should choose your stories carefully, because that window of opportunity limits your candidates significantly. Write a story worth writing, and worth reading. That's the key to an ultimate storytelling experience.

Ask yourself if your premise appeals to a wide and inherently commercial readership. Or does it focus too narrowly on a specific corner of life, even if that issue is important to you? While it's not impossible for stellar execution to elevate an unlikely story to greatness, the odds are forever in the favor of stories that deliver precisely what the genre promises its readers. In either case, concept and premise are like a marquee, giving readers some indication that they will find compatible tastes and fascinations inside.

Don't make a genre story overly driven by or dependent on your characters. Don't assume readers care about your characters before you give them a reason to care. Don't force absurdity into your premise for the sake of originality. Don't bend the rules of reason or the odds of coincidence to make your premise work. We place our bets when we make choices about these elements.

A story crossed my desk recently in which the President of the United States, in conjunction with a whacked-out military zealot, sets out to destroy entire American cities to illustrate our country's inability to deal with tragedy, and pins the attacks on foreign terrorists. Definitely conceptual, and yet so far out there that hardly anyone would give the story serious consideration. The author's story sensibility was the problem, despite having a narrative arc that actually executed the idea rather well. The author believed this was an A-grade concept and premise; my feedback was that agents and editors would not agree. After reflection, which included a thorough review of the concept and premise for his story, the author ultimately dropped the project entirely, saving perhaps a year of his writing life and allowing him to start his next project with a more informed sense of the craft.

The whole thing, therefore, ended up being a win rather than a rejection. There is always something to learn from these experiences.

Write what you please, but know that readers are reading what *they* please as well.

A SECOND PASS AT GRADING YOUR STORY

In these last two chapters, you have discovered and explored the nature and inherent power of concept *and* premise. In doing so, your writing world—and indeed, your story—may already look quite different. Now it's time to revisit your story's raw grist and see how your heightened awareness of the role of concept and premise has changed how you grade it. If your concept wasn't solid the first time, and if your premise failed to meet the criteria for a robust story, this round may be a wakeup call of epic proportions across all twelve variables of the core competencies and their story physics. Using the definitions and criteria provided thus far, return to those twelve story elements and grade your execution in particular, and your understanding in general, once again.

You may, in this very process, discover what is holding your story back.

STORY ELEMENT OR ESSENCE	GRADE (A–F)
1. Concept (the presence of something conceptual)	
2. Dramatic premise/arc (hero's quest, goal)	
3. Dramatic tension (conflict via antagonistic element)	
4. Vicarious reader experience	
5. Compelling characterization	
6. Reader empathy (what the reader roots for)	
7. Thematic weight, relevance, and resonance	
8. Effective story architecture (structure)	
9. Optimal pacing	
10. Scene execution	
11. Writing voice	
12. Narrative strategy	

THE VALUE OF YOUR SELF-ASSESSMENT

The collision of old awareness with a new and enlightened consciousness will define the future of your story. Because if you refuse to change a story you believe is an A on all counts but is really a C (or worse) based on the criteria, then your revision will fall short. The entire point here is discovery and *change* … fixing, upgrading, strengthening. There's nowhere to go but up. If you believed you were already on top of the mountain—and thus that those who rejected you were just plain wrong—you may have realized that *you're* the one who was wrong after all.

This realization is cause for celebration, because, as is the case in any sort of rehabilitation effort, you can't begin the growth process until you acknowledge the problems. Now you are about to learn what is required to make your story better.

THE KEY TO EVERYTHING

The human body has a brain. All bodily functions, every last one of them, are controlled by this organ. The brain directs not only the functions of the body but also the presentation of the person to the world—his appearance, his choices, his talents and shortcomings, his worldview, his ability to love, his propensity for darkness, his moral compass. His entire being stems from whatever is going on within his brain, as formed by his experiences, surroundings, and exterior influences.

Your story has a brain, too. It is the determinant of everything that happens and is perceived within the story. That organ, if you will, is your *premise*, which we discussed at length in the previous chapter. And as a brain benefits from a good upbringing and an education, your premise benefits greatly when a strong conceptual context resides at its core.

Your premise, influenced by the power of your concept, completely controls the story: contextually, materially, sequentially, cosmetically, thematically, dramatically. But notice that it is *not* the full story, which requires a plethora of events and catalysts to create a cohesive flow. Rather, the premise hits the high marks, and the story is left to the manuscript. Premise is a planning *and* a pitching tool, defining your intentions for the story and the promise you are making to readers. Further details are the stuff of outlines, or exploratory drafts, both of which are extensions of the premise itself.

You might be wondering this: *So if concept and premise are simply summaries of what awaits in a story, what constitutes the story itself? What are the actual ingredients of a manuscript?*

You've already encountered these ingredients in the grading exercises you've completed so far. You've graded your concept and your premise and then projected those changes across the arc of the story, with grades given on that evolved story arc. But ten other story elements and essences, which are forthcoming in the next two chapters, remain to be defined and used as benchmarks for a successful story. These are the building blocks that you put on the page, and what you may consider revising.

This brings us to a crossroads that doubles as a paradox. Those other elements and essences don't stand a chance if the premise itself comes up short or is already compromised. They are nothing more than parts and piles, waiting for order. Premise is that order.

Premise doesn't explain *how* things happen in your story. It is merely a summary of intention. And while it remains the most empowering of all the story elements and essences—you have no story without a premise, and thus it is essential—it is only the first step in creating a novel or screenplay. It is the *vision* for the story, without which you end up in chaos, hosting a wrestling match between your ideas and inspiration. And therein we stumble upon what might have been the undoing of your manuscript.

THE SEARCH FOR STORY

Just possibly your premise wasn't clear when you began writing. It wasn't *finished*. The draft you wrote from that incomplete premise became, in effect, *a search for the story,* and when you found it somewhere along that road—if you found it at all—you proceeded from that point without returning to the first page armed with this newly discovered context.

Searching for the story while you're writing it is like setting out from Seattle for a drive to … well, you're not sure. You just head east. Or south. Wherever the road takes you. So you drive, and the scenery is indeed gorgeous for a while. But then you begin thinking about where this road is taking you, so you try out a few options. You change freeways in Denver and head south. But it's too hot in New Mexico, and you don't know anybody there. So you head east into Texas and then up through Oklahoma toward Chicago. You're still not sure where this trip will end up. But you never reach Chicago because somewhere in Kansas you decide you want to lie on a beach in Miami. Yeah, that sounds good; let's go there. So you break out a map on your smart phone and plot the best course to Florida, and off you go.

All of this is fine if you're alone, or if taking in the scenery is your only purpose, or if you have no reason for the drive other than killing time with interesting pit stops. But when you're writing a novel or a screenplay, you are not alone; the objective isn't the scenery. You're driving a bus loaded with readers who bought a ticket based on your promise via the premise. If you've been searching for the story this whole time, they're not sure of the destination. But now you can finally tell them, twenty hours and two hundred pages into the journey: You're heading full steam toward Miami. But … is your current story, the one that isn't sure what it is, the best way, the most rewarding way, the most dramatic way, to reach Miami?

It probably isn't. Because in a story that works, every page is written in context to the author's full and informed knowledge of how that page fits into a bigger picture. In fact, if that bigger picture is still fuzzy, the journey has been chaos up until the moment you decided where you were going after all. And now, suddenly, you're in a hurry—you finally have a *plot*—so you rush into it. Sure, you gave your passengers some good times, but this is supposed to be commercial travel, not the whimsy of the driver. And so the trip itself is judged a disaster. It takes eight days to complete a four-day journey. When you translate that experience on paper, other routes from Seattle to Miami suddenly look more appealing, scenery included.

That's what happens when you use your draft as a tool, applied within your process, to find your best story, and then actually submit that draft with the word *Final* stamped on it somewhere. When you find your best story—this, too, is an outcome determined solely by the astuteness of your story sensibility—you need to start another draft, or at least revise the current chaotic draft to the extent that it seems like a new draft, in context to the discovered destination and route.

That new, concise plan, developed based on a known big picture and destination, in all likelihood *will* work. Or it will at least work better than the draft written without that clarity. That is the plan you need to develop and polish.

Hear me clearly: I'm not dumping on a process that uses drafts to search for and find the story. However you search for it, if the process works for you, it is a good thing. But here's what happens to too many writers, too often: They don't revise their current draft or write a new one once they land on a story in the *middle* of that search draft. They keep the initial segment of the draft, the pages that are without context to the newly discovered core story, with all its side trips and unplanned stops and breakdowns and dead ends, and proceed from that point with a more informed context, labeling it a *final* draft that merely has a focused back end (now that the author has finally found the story) and a front end that never really knew where the story was headed.

If that's you—you may already be squirming as you read this—take heart. This chapter will give you guidelines and criteria that will help you focus on creating the best story possible, the one you promised in your premise, regardless of how you searched for your story.

First and foremost, you need to get that premise right.

Sometimes it takes a chaotic draft to get there, in which case you end up with a new and better premise for the effort. But nonetheless, you need a *final* premise, one that meets all of the requisite criteria and standards (see the previous chapter), and then—wait for it, because this is the critical moment—you *stick to that core story.*

That's the goal: a solid, compelling, dramatic core story. And it begins with a premise that earns those same adjectives.

When you have a criteria-meeting premise, you *know* your core dramatic story from the first page, at least in terms of the four major structural parts told in sequence, separated by five major story milestones that render it dramatic, evolving, and satisfying. You know that it is the best core story available: one that fulfills the promise made by the premise.

Can that core story change? Certainly it can. Within the draft you may find an even better twist or context for the story, which, when adopted, actually shifts the premise as well. Premise and core story are the same things; when you change one, you change the other.

HOW TO SCREW UP YOUR PREMISE WITHIN A DRAFT

Let me count the ways. There are dozens of them, but they can be grouped into toxic categories of story killers that murder a huge percentage of submitted manuscripts. I know this because I've culled this data from my database of hundreds of dissected and analyzed unpublished stories submitted to me for story coaching over the past three years. And usually I can spot this fatal flaw right there in the premise, which I always ask for prior to the read.

See the case studies at the end of this book to see how these dark missteps gobble up the stories they appear in, despite the best intentions of their authors.

Rejection is all but guaranteed when you are guilty of the following storytelling sins. For each, I include an example of a story that commits this sin, as well as a solution for revising the story killer in question.

1. You change lanes in the middle.

Your concept currently defines a reasonably compelling story arena. We're in; it sounds great. And yet, the story never goes deep into this arena, or doesn't stay there, or doesn't leverage the compelling power of the arena originally granted to your premise. For example, your concept promises a story in which a character uses paranormal gifts to make dreams come true and read minds at will. And yet within the story, while your hero has that talent, and while she may use it from time to time, it never surfaces as a catalyst for a core story that depends on it, which was the promise of the premise itself. In a broken story, that original conceptual notion doesn't remain at the core of the story's spine; the story takes a twist and becomes something else. It's like a bad sweater: It's just there, unseen and unworn in the bottom drawer, exerting no story influence whatsoever.

This issue also crops up at the premise level. You promise a story that is about a woman finding her lost mother because she can't stand the thought of her dying alone. There's also an inheritance at stake. That's the crux of the premise. Then, in the middle of the story, she meets a guy and falls in love, but he's married. Suddenly the story is all about *that*. The quest to find the mother fades into the distance in favor of a doomed love story. It's a different story now, and not the one promised in the premise. It's a lane change, and it'll get your story rejected faster than that bad sweater at a debutante ball.

The fix is to connect any new plotlines to the original core story, making the new ones dependent upon the core. In the last example, the woman may have to choose between this blooming new love and the search for her mother. She must be willing to walk away from the guy if he doesn't accept that she needs the freedom to pursue the search. The love story then becomes integral to the original core story, adding tension and urgency in the process. The mistake is to abandon the core story to pursue another avenue; the fix is to connect any new avenues back to the original core story.

The inability to stay focused on a core story is one of the leading story killers. Changing lanes in the middle might have been the cause of your rejection. If you think that's the case, you now have the awareness to fix your story with a strategic, creative, brilliant redesign of your premise to accommodate the new idea. If not, perhaps you should trash the new plotlines altogether and stick to your original vision.

2. The story relies exclusively on an internal antagonist (personal demon) as the source of conflict.

Poor Beth. She's unhappy. Her dad was an abusive schmuck, and as an adult Beth is hooking up with men just like him as she looks for approval and some sort of sick closure. *Yes, I can make him love me, if it doesn't kill me first.* Man after man crosses her path (meaning you're already relying on another lethal story killer, the *episodic* narrative spine). Nothing stands in the way of Beth's happiness other than her inability to deal with her past, and nothing is stopping her from dealing with it. Yet, all we see in the story is one more schmuck dealing another cruel blow to her, and then she's off to look for another loser, unhappier than before.

Her resolution? She wakes up one day and gets it. With a bolt of awareness, an epiphany of clarity, she decides she's tired of hurting. So she fires that internal demon, sends it packing. Suddenly she's going to be okay. The end. We were with her all the way.

That story doesn't stand a chance. To revise this premise, you need to give the character a specific external goal to pursue (a story of how one man's love could heal her), and something standing in her way (the guy is a priest). The thing that stands in her way must be *external*, a catalyst that creates a new awareness within her, and it must summon her inner demons. Once they surface, they are confronted, defeated, and banished. The character can't just have a sudden, unmotivated realization. She needs to take steps to beat down her demons before she can create her own salvation by *doing* something, achieving something, or reaching a specific, definable goal.

Stories that simply chronicle a sequence of dark episodes, linked only by some internal demon and not in context to a solution or outcome, just don't work. If this is your story, you need a better one that leverages your hero's demons by showing them getting in her way while she's focusing on a critical goal. You need a *plot*, not a diary of misery.

3. The resolution comes out of nowhere.

Having a character bolt upright in a moment of clarity is the worst possible resolution to a story. It's right up there with having your hero read someone's mind to learn the liberating truth, and it's almost as bad as ending with a fist fight in which the hero knocks the villain senseless, a situation made even more ridiculous when the hero is a fourteen-year-old and the villain is a fifty-year-old ex-Marine.

That story crossed my desk recently. A young girl knocked the combat-toughened villain out with one punch, then lived happily ever after.

Another common mistake in this realm is the sudden materialization of an unexpected, unforeshadowed, and unlikely catalyst for the hero's ability to resolve the story. Like, the ghost of the hero's father appears before him in his darkest hour to assure him "You can do it, kid." (That, too, recently came across my desk.)

Yes, the hero needs to be the catalyst for the ending, the primary mechanism of the ending, and he can indeed be summoned through the trial and error and growth we've seen over the course of the story (in other words, the character arc). But even then, the hero must do something, not be told to do something or stumble upon some sudden unlikely coincidence or good fortune (sometimes known as a *deus ex machina*, which translates to "God from the machine." Leave God out of it and your ending will work better.)

The fix is to show a resolution that is put into motion by something the hero *does*, as a product of who he is now, a product of courage and growth, with cleverness and strength and willpower, rather than something the hero simply realizes. He can realize that action is required, but it is that action, not the realization of the need for it, that becomes the catalyst for the story's resolution.

4. Your hero is *saved* rather than saving himself.

Your hero cannot merely *observe* the story's resolution from the sidelines. He cannot be rescued. Rather, he must save himself by outwitting, outplaying, and outlasting a villain with an antagonistic agenda.

Here's an example of how this mistake looks. The story is about a woman seeking to prove her son's innocence in a murder case. The newly elected district attorney is after the son, cutting corners and hiding evidence to make himself look good. The police are in his pocket, and her son's only hope is his mother. At the end, her hard work has gained the sympathy of a local reporter, who unearths new evidence that not only proves her son is innocent but also nails the corrupt D.A. for fabricating evidence. She's grateful and ends up sleeping with the reporter, and they fall in love.

That's a terrible ending. Any new evidence unearthed, any proof of her son's innocence, needs to be the direct result of her own heroic efforts rather than luck or, even worse, someone else's actions.

5. Your premise is a life story.

Backstory is a beautiful thing, but an entire novel that serves as nothing other than a venue to reveal backstory is doomed. That only works when the story is both true and amazing. Your novel needs a singular dramatic spine from which the events unfold in the story's current time frame.

Stories like this come from writers who forget they are writing within a genre and try to write a character-driven literary masterpiece. Character is drummed into us from the very beginning of our writing journey, and without the proper understanding, newer writers might overplay that element to the detriment of dramatic tension. That's what happened to a writer I recently met with at a conference during a story review session. The pitch was good, and he had a massively powerful inciting incident—one that served as the story's first plot point—that, after setting things up, would ignite the dramatic spine of the story. I asked him when that happened, what page it was on in the manuscript. He said page 290. I asked him how long the book was, and he said it was 410 pages. When I asked him why he was violating the core principles of structure to present a setup that was well over halfway into the narrative, instead of the optimal location of the 20th to 25th percentile, he said he wanted to nail the hero, to fully flesh him out using backstory and a vivid picture of his life before the hammer dropped. When I told him this was a fatal structural flaw, one driven by his over-weighing of the function of character within his story—which was a thriller, by the way—he didn't know what to think. Then he said it had been rejected eight times already, and then I just looked at him. Silence reigned. Then I suggested he bone up on the principles of structure and the tropes of the thriller in general and sent him away with specific resources to do just that. He'd ruined a perfectly good premise by not knowing how to execute it ... in this case, by allowing character to trump dramatic tension, within a genre that lives and dies by the level of its conceptually driven drama.

Another way writers shoot their manuscripts in the foot in this regard is to deliberately, as the core of their concept and premise, set out to tell the life story of a fictional hero. This results in a series of anecdotal, periodic, episodic sections, not unlike a collection of short stories that feature the hero in all of them, without a central dramatic spine that gives the hero something to do, a reason to do it (stakes), something blocking that effort, with threat and urgency exerting pressure all the while, within a vicariously delicious setting and situation. The fix for this? Go back to the drawing board and learn to write a novel. Discover how the novels in your genre are conceived, structured, and resolved relative to both dramatic arc and character arc. In other words, learn the basics of novel writing.

Sometimes the writer just isn't ready. Sometimes the story is bigger than the writer's ability to pull it off. Both reasons explain a significant percentage of rejections. The save is easy: Learn the craft from square one. You can't invent how a novel unfolds; that's a universal model, a given. Rather, you can invent how your story unfolds *within* those parameters, freeing you to be as creative and focused as you choose ... as long as you don't color outside the lines of the basic principles of storytelling.

Malcolm Gladwell says in his bestseller *Outliers* that it takes ten thousand hours of apprenticeship to finally master a professional endeavor at the level required to compete with other professionals. If you've ever wondered what is going on during those ten thousand hours, this is it: the discovery, exploration, and practice of the craft itself: submitting to it, embracing it, and owning it … rather than trying to invent unique structures and principles outside of an awareness of what has been established and in play for thousands of years.

6. You've resorted to episodic storytelling.

Your hero and his friend go to Italy after graduating from college. One guy loses his passport, and the American embassy must intervene. Then they go to France, where they get in a bar fight. Then they go to London and get laid. Then they go to Spain and lie on a beach for a month, drinking too much. Then they come home and find real jobs. The end.

That's one heckuva story if you lived it. But as a novel, it's a complete bust. There is zero dramatic tension. The trip has no stakes. Nothing blocks the characters' path toward a goal, because they have no goal. It is a collection of memories and short stories, which do not a novel make. Ever.

The fix is to create a central issue—a problem to solve, an opportunity to seek, or some other milestone the hero needs to pursue and achieve to avoid dark consequences or achieve something wonderful. Place that central event amidst the sequence of other episodes you long to share in the story, or use some of those as backstory. Don't confuse a travelogue, a memoir, or a documentary with a novel—they are different things. Episodic tales without that central dramatic spine—the hero needing or wanting something and setting out to get it—are documentaries, except that they aren't true.

Again, this is an example of a novel written before its time, by a writer who has rushed his learning curve, committing to a flawed story premise before he understands how the work is actually done, how stories are best told at a professional level.

It's sad but simple: Many manuscripts fail because their authors don't fully know what they're doing yet. They don't know the difference between a concept and a premise. They don't understand the role of dramatic tension in a story. They don't grasp the role of character within a story, believing that character is everything and that plot is optional.

The fix is to keep hiking up the learning curve by immersing yourself in the realm of craft. If you're reading this, you're on that path already. Keep going. The true key to fixing your story awaits on this journey, by finally wrapping your head around the core principles and their execution.

7. You've attempted to feature more than one protagonist.

Trying to include more than one hero may be your undoing. There are exceptions to this, but your own sagging manuscript may be a case of biting off more than you can chew. Ensemble stories call for very advanced storytelling craft, with an underlying sense of meaning and ultimate stakes. Those stories are out there, and if you've encountered them and found yourself seduced, then this might explain your intention to write one yourself. But know that you're diving into the deep end of the pool, taking on one of the most challenging forms in fiction, and you need significant experience and chops to pull it off. If you've failed, the simple explanation might be that you're not ready for it. Again, the fix is to make yourself ready by immersing yourself in craft and studying successful stories that do manage to pull this off.

A more immediate fix is to reduce the focus of the story to a single protagonist, perhaps with sidekicks and lesser characters who are attached to and have roles within that main dramatic spine. This brings you back into the realm of classic structure and expositional principles, all of which are available for your consumption and adoption.

At most you should consider using two main characters. And if you try it, don't simply unspool their stories in parallel, without having them develop a meaningful connection that becomes ironic and changes everything. Make sure each character engages in a singular plot. One way to make this work is to have the two main characters end up as lovers, or partners of some type, both seeking the same thing as they face the same antagonists and situations. Complications ensue when their unified goals begin to differ, or if they are at odds in other aspects of their relationship. *The Night Circus* by Erin Morgenstern is such a novel, with two main characters who occupy the position of protagonists in the story, but they're also dueling magicians who end up falling in love. The possibilities are numerous, and Morgenstern explores many of them with a master's touch. Reading stories that demonstrate how complex narratives work is one of the more powerful and efficient ways to internalize the forms and functions required to make it all run elegantly and effectively, with emotional resonance and compelling drama.

Remember, this rogue's gallery of story killers assumes you had a workable premise in the first place.

The key word is *workable*. Sure, a premise that calls for, say, six protagonists on a shared journey into darkness to save their entire village seems like a good idea at the time, but when you commit to such a proposition, you are making a promise to deliver. But you might just be writing checks you can't cash at this point in your writing journey, and your story sensibility isn't yet at the level to stop it before it becomes a train wreck on the page.

Again, it all comes back to story sensibility. It drives what you conceive as a premise, and it defines your ability to flesh it out across the arc of the novel. Too often the fix is simply to ramp up your skills and your experience, leading to an evolved sense of story that allows you to create stronger premises and provides the know-how to pull them off. If you're staring at a rejection slip, or if you sense your novel isn't working well enough, it's good to sniff out the specifics of what is causing that verdict ... but it's better to become the writer who knows enough to avoid those same mistakes.

This is where rejection, or the need to revise a story you want to save, becomes a blessing in disguise. Because it initiates an opportunity not only to save the story but also to build your skills and sensibilities in the process, leading toward a more intuitive access to creative intentions and decisions that are doable and real rather than residing above your pay grade as a new or less than fully enlightened writer.

These examples may have all begun as solid premises. Or not. Maybe the story was terminal at the premise stage, and nothing you could do via execution could save it. These stories failed to live up to the promise of their premises, or they died trying.

But there are many ways a story can fail at the premise level when the key criteria of an effective premise is missing or misplayed. The story may have little or no inherent potential for dramatic tension. It may lack a compelling plot, because it lacks a natural antagonist or villain. Perhaps the story relies on "real life" to present obstacles to the hero's quest, which often leads to episodic narrative without a central spine. Or there may be nothing much at stake other than the hero's happiness, redemption, or the restoration of self-confidence.

In genre fiction especially, you need a *plot*.

These loose threads may indeed be presented as premises, but they are weak premises, almost impossible to pull off without the narrative skills of Joyce Carol Oates (which means, either by intention or default, you are working within the literary fiction genre) and a floor full of story editors chipping in on multiple drafts.

That isn't an option these days. Rather, you'll simply get rejected and be forced to move on. Where you go from there—another fruitless submission, or a revision that strengthens the story—is totally your call.

Broken is broken, no matter how many times you submit the work. The better bet, almost always, is to look for ways to revise the story before another submission. If you have credible feedback to work from, then this is your only rational choice.

As I've said before, the only stories that succeed in finding an agent or a publisher after an initial rejection or a wave of criticism are ones that simply didn't appeal to that particular reader (the one doing the rejecting). Agents are readers, and all readers have preferences. Your story simply may not have been one they preferred.

Poor execution, however, will always get you rejected.

Or it could be that your story doesn't fit with their current roster of clients, projects, and publishing slots. There is a jungle full of reasons writers get rejected, and sometimes it's simply a matter of "the wrong place at the wrong time."

And then there are the ravenous predators lurking in that jungle, waiting to devour your story whole and spit it back to you in shreds. Those are the story killers you've just encountered, and they are creations of your own making.

Maybe you recognize these toxic choices in the work you are on the cusp of revising. If you do, you're one of the lucky ones; it bodes well for the state of your story sensibilities, especially if that awareness has dawned here, within the embrace of this book. Because now you *know*. What you didn't recognize as risky is now clearly something you understand and can recognize, which is the first and best step toward repair. You have tools—definitions, target criteria, benchmarks, and comparative examples—that can elevate you to a higher level, beginning at the point at which you conceive a concept and land on a premise. You can then execute that story across a dramatic arc lasting about four hundred pages or so.

Allow me to bottom-line this for you.

You need to know your core story. Not a bunch of threads leading to something unclear and irresolvable. You need to unspool that story along a core dramatic spine, a linear sequence of setup, twist, response, and revelation, more twists, proactive response, and yet more revelation. You need an antagonistic force (usually a villain) seeking to block your hero's path, then another major twist that sets the hero toward an inevitable confrontation, perhaps with a final shocking twist that allows the hero to confront the villain and resolve the goal, one way or another.

And here's the kicker: All of this concerns a *singular* core story. The one you promised in your premise. The one that met all those criteria for effectiveness. The one empowered by an underlying conceptual context.

No slice-of-life stories. No "adventures of …" stories. No episodic ramblings. No plotless character profiles, especially life stories of fictional protagonists. No life-sucks-then-you-die diaries of miserable people.

Of course, to avoid all of these pitfalls you need to understand what they are. Perhaps you didn't before. So be grateful that your rejected or doubted story has led you here, because now you know. Or at least you are on the cusp of knowing.

Your readers want hope. They want to be engaged, and they want to be emotionally involved. They want to empathize, to root for something. They want to be scared, and they want to root against something. They want a vicarious ride, to feel as if they are in the story. They want to feel the weight of the story's stakes and the urgency of the pursuit of resolution. They want to relate to it, even if they can't. They want to feel, to laugh and to cry and to lose themselves. To be entertained, moved, changed, enraged, terrified, turned on, and seduced. They want to fall in love again. They want to live within your pages.

Does your story accomplish these feats? Does your premise create a vehicle that can deliver all of this? Only your story sensibility can tell you, or at least make an educated guess. Which makes your sense of story the most fertile ground to access a higher level of storytelling acumen.

If you're not there yet, if you can't recognize what went wrong and where to take the story next, then you aren't done. Maybe it isn't a lack of storytelling chops; maybe the story itself isn't strong enough to house all of these elements and essences. Story conception and story execution are two different facets of your story sensibility, and maybe one of them is stronger than the other. Maybe you haven't found your best story yet. You need to go deeper and wider, think outside of your box, and take some risks. And yet, you need to play within the lines of the genre and adhere to the highest principles of fiction.

Those highest principles can be boiled down to this: Drama and conflict are everything. In a field in which we hear that character is everything, this is actually not a contradiction. Drama and conflict give your character something to *do*. They are the catalysts that allow character to emerge. They are the forces of story, the things that put story into motion. Without them your story dies. It's that simple.

In the next two chapters, we'll look at those other ten story elements and essences you graded earlier. But keep in mind that they totally depend on the strength and viability of the *premise* they are executing, as empowered by whatever conceptual energy you've imparted to it.

We're about to move from story-level viability into the realm of expositional narrative *craft*. Of execution. And believe me, the realm of craft is another jungle full of story killers. They are mistakes and miscues of a diffcrent species, ones that can surreptitiously tear the heart out of your story, or, at the very least, cause it to underachieve.

If you don't *know*.

Let's make sure you do.

NARRATIVE BODYBUILDING PART ONE

I love the analogy of bodybuilding in context to story fixing.

In the human body, the process of building strength involves working the muscle to the point where it begins to break down; connective tissue actually tears when you lift weights. These torn muscles quickly repair, only now they are slightly stronger than before to handle what the body perceives to be a demand for increased strength.

That's just what we're doing here: breaking your existing draft down with the goal of growing it back even stronger. Only it won't be slightly stronger—more like "on steroids" stronger.

IT'S ALL IN YOUR HEAD

The brain can continue to live when the body is rendered dysfunctional. This analogy teaches us that even a story with a solid concept and premise can be rendered incapable of movement and full life due to poor execution.

But, other than by artificial means, the body cannot live when the brain goes dark. Everything dies. As I've said before, premise is essentially the brain of your story, driven by concept. When the concept and premise don't work, no amount of genius, including your stellar prose, applied to the other core competencies and realms of story physics can save it.

In this chapter and the next, we will examine the definitions and criteria for the major story elements and essences. The goal is recognition and acknowledgment in context to the story revision process. These two chapters will allow you to see, perhaps for the first time, how your execution has compromised the promise of your premise. Or, on the flip side, how even your best swing at it failed to breathe life into a premise that was stumbling out of the starting gate.

The previous three chapters were a seminar on concept and premise, together becoming the brain trust of your story, the core source of its potential relative to a reader's perception of intrigue, drama, and vicarious experience within your story world. If that hasn't jelled, I encourage you to return to those chapters and stay there until it finally clicks, because everything depends on it. The source of your story's weakness, and, thus, the focus of your revision, may be rooted in problems with concept, premise, or both. You may not have found your best story yet.

If concept and premise aren't the problem, if both stand up to their respective criteria and are judged as commercially viable by those who possess a proven story sensibility, then these next chapters may hold the key to fixing your story. You may need to open yourself to the possibility—the probability—that despite a great story idea, your execution could be better.

DRAMATIC TENSION

As a story coach I see this all the time, especially with genre-centered stories: The concept is compelling, the premise promises a great ride … and then the writer seems to step over the heart of the premise to focus on character almost exclusively, dwelling too much on backstory, marching the protagonist through an episodic sequence of life experiences that do not clearly connect to a dramatic spine, the one promised by that killer premise. Sure, we get to know that character intimately, but until your hero is doing something in pursuit of a goal, the picture isn't complete.

The engine of fiction is not character. You'll hear that it is, but this doesn't clarify a deeper truth. Character is critical, but it isn't the main source of energy within a story.

Conflict fuels a story. In any genre other than literary fiction, conflict is the *source* of character. You need to give your character a challenge, a need, something to do, something with a purpose, something with stakes, and then layer in an antagonistic force—a villain—who seeks to block the quest or path of your hero. Without that quest your story becomes a biographical, diary-like episodic sequence. And without conflict you have overlooked the most important element in any story, including literary fiction: dramatic tension.

DRAMATIC TENSION DEFINED

It's simple, really. Your story poses a question. One answer serves your hero's goals, while others thwart it. Whatever threatens the hero's goals, the object of his quest, is an antagonistic force. That force—usually a villain—proactively blocks the hero's path in any way possible. (Some stories use nonhuman antagonists, like weather or disease or government oppression, but the dynamics are the same.) When the hero fights back against the antagonist, heroically finding a way to overcome the obstacles, that confrontation is fraught with conflict that creates dramatic tension, because the reader is rooting for and caring about the hero's overall goal *and* the outcome of any specific threat, confrontational moment, doubt, or lurking danger.

The *source* of your reader's emotional engagement is dramatic tension stemming from conflict. This is conflict that arises from the core thread of the story—drama you have created because *stakes* are attached. That experience is tense for the hero and tense for the reader rooting for that hero. Without dramatic tension, your story will be static, and before long it will die.

The Core Story

In the previous chapters we learned about the importance of understanding your core story. Not the backstory, not the inner demons of the hero, not the subplots, not the various episodic side trips and experiences and dreams of the story, but the core dramatic spine, first and foremost. A novel that jumps from one dramatic question to another, none of which arise from the core story, is problematic and will be quickly rejected. This alone may explain your rejection, and if so you may now know what to do about it: Respin the narrative around a single dramatic pursuit that takes front-and-center priority throughout the arc of the story. Because you are telling *that* story.

The core drama constitutes the hero's pursuit of a solution to a specific threat or problem, and/or the quest to seize an opportunity. Either of those has consequences, which is the source of reader empathy. The core story poses a dramatic question, generically stated as this: "Will the hero achieve X?" with X standing in for what the hero needs or wants. If X doesn't happen, it will yield dark consequences.

Lisa needs a kidney for her child. Her philandering husband lost his job, and they've lost their health insurance. The child has a rare blood type. They have recently arrived in the United States from a third-world country and have no relatives or friends. In fact, they're in the country illegally.

This is a riveting premise because the stakes are so high and the opposition to the wife's goal so dire. The reader will care about this, at least if she has a beating heart and a soul, and especially if the writer has drawn the characters vividly and sympathetically. The reader roots for a positive outcome and remains captivated because the route to the end is not obvious. Lisa must do something to create a positive outcome, and her efforts will be heroic.

That's the dramatic setup. But we're not done yet. It's certainly a dark and antagonistic situation, but there is no villain yet, no bad guy. So let's create one.

When Lisa goes to a local government agency for help, she reveals that she is in the country illegally. The case officer is a by-the-book, cold-blooded bitch who is prejudiced and angered by undocumented citizens being in "her country." And so she makes it her personal mission to not only prevent Lisa from getting a dime of government assistance but also to have her and her daughter deported as soon as possible.

Now you have a core story—not just a profile of Lisa and her situation but something Lisa must *do*. A plot. Anything other than a focus on this plot hits the pause button on the core storyline and is therefore a diversion. Too much backstory and too many subplots detract from the energy of the core plot and the emotional resonance for the reader. She has an important mission—a quest—before her. A villain blocks her path. The clock is ticking as her daughter's condition becomes grimmer by the day. And while she has a sympathetic doctor who helps the poor, that guy can't solve the core story problem because the evil government case worker is waiting to shut down the physician's practice if he even sneezes in that direction. And if Lisa falls for the doctor … well, that would make a nice subplot, but including this is a bad idea if it takes over the novel, changing lanes from the former core plot to a new one featuring the doctor as a love interest. Such a subplot needs to serve the core story spine, not distract from it.

This balancing of core story and subplot is a skill set, one that can either get you published or explain why you were rejected. When writers try to give equal—or even too much—attention to a subplot, even when it involves the hero, everything slows down. Balance doesn't mean equal airtime; it means maintaining the core story as the primary narrative and then artfully weaving in any subplots in a manner that adds to either reader empathy or dramatic tension, or both.

The core story creates the primary source of dramatic tension. In this case, it needs to be a plotline that isn't just a focus on a character but rather allows the character to emerge, face her demons, and summon her true strength, genius, and motherly ferocity with courage. The plot becomes the catalyst for character to emerge.

If your story is character focused to the extent that readers have trouble finding or engaging with a core *dramatic* story unfolding in the story's present time—a plot—give them something more to root for. Readers can't root for the past, via backstory. A backstory is what it is, and readers can't hope for it to change. But they will root for a drama set in the present that engulfs the hero, and that should be the focus of your core storyline. Readers won't simply be observing, which is what character-centric stories with a lot of backstory ask them to do, because the character in the present tense is all they have. If you have discovered that your story is too character driven, or that it lacks a core story and therefore dramatic tension, then you may have just found its Achilles' heel. Now you have something to fix, something to revise. Now you have hope.

Using the expectations and tropes of your chosen genre as a guideline (meaning that your romance novel shouldn't have a mystery as its core story; it needs to be a *romance*), you develop and focus on a dramatic spine told in the present. This core story asks a compelling dramatic question and elicits reader empathy and support with a hero's goal that is blocked by a villain or antagonist. Pressure and urgency are in play, and, most of all, stakes drive both sides of the race to attain the goal.

Inner Needs as Core Story Motivation

It's time to define your core story. What does your hero want and need? What blocks his quest to attain it, and what is at stake?

If your answer is "inner peace" or "happiness," or another vague or ambiguous term, it's likely not strong enough. Your character needs an *external* quest, something to find and engage with, to defeat or achieve—whatever is required to succeed in that quest. When your character overcomes the *external* quest, *then* he'll have happiness and peace, which is wonderful. But that isn't the same as a core story quest with happiness and peace as the primary stakes. Happiness is the desired *outcome*, not the dramatic stakes. You'll need to generate an external means and strategy that create a goal, which, if reached, will allow him to access and embrace the inner peace he seeks. In that context, inner peace is the goal, not the means. And a core story is always about means, because a core story is always about what *happens*, not just what the outcome is. Internal growth and satisfaction work best as the results of the quest, not the path the hero treads to get there.

I encourage you to read that last part again, because so many writers—newer writers in particular, who have a high vision for a story that deals with psychological healing—get it wrong. They try to make the search for happiness the road, when in fact it is better positioned as the destination. The better story focuses on the journey itself.

Be clear on this: The core story is about what the character needs *to do and accomplish* to obtain peace and happiness.

Maybe your view of your core story has already changed based on this chapter alone. So let's see. Right now, on a separate sheet of paper, define your core story.

The Core Dramatic Question

Determining the core dramatic question is easy if you nail down the core story. The question will be some form of this: Will the hero succeed in the quest as defined by the core story? Will she defeat the villain and overcome the odds against her?

It's easy to overthink the core dramatic question, but it's actually often simplistic, despite a core story that is anything but. It boils down to success or failure. The stakes determine the degree to which readers will engage emotionally, which translates to the degree to which they root for the successful outcome in context to the degree to which they fear for the safety and well-being of the hero based on the consequences of failure. This is precisely why characterization is so critical, and yet it supports my contention that character is driven by, and thus subordinate to, a compelling core story question. Plot gives the hero something to do and the reader something to root for. That's the whole ballgame right there, also in simplistic, yet almost unfailing, terms.

In our last example, the core dramatic question is: Will Lisa find a kidney for her ill daughter in time to save her? Will she thwart the efforts of the evil case worker to have her deported?

The answer is either yes or no—or some surprise-twist hybrid of the two. The plot is deep and layered, but the dramatic question isn't. It comes down to win or lose.

Knowing this clarifies the author's primary job: to suck readers into the hero's quest on multiple levels, make them live and feel the journey itself, make them fear or respect the consequences (stakes) that drive it all, make them fear and loathe the villain, and make them hang on every scene—because they have been made to care about the hero—so they can see how it turns out. That recipe is as old as paper itself and just as powerful today as it has ever been.

It's amazing, really, when you consider the obvious simplicity of the author's task, which truly never varies, versus the complexity of pulling it off over three or four hundred pages. This explains why multiple drafts are almost always involved. It also explains the need for revision: Somehow, the author—either unwittingly or in ignorant defiance—has departed from that prescribed path.

The magic of a core question is in its unspoken next step: *How will she do this?* Your job is to make readers care about this question. They are rooting for her. They have empathy for her plight because they can relate to it. That's the math: concern for the character, plus fear and engagement with any jeopardy that confronts someone you care about. Readers immerse themselves in this journey as if it were their own. They *feel* it. They fear and despise the wicked case worker in our example story. They hear the ticking clock. They dry the tears of Lisa's frightened daughter. They hug Lisa in the dead of night as she weeps in the bed of a government-funded high-rise apartment building, where a friend—a minor character created to give Lisa a shoulder to cry on and act as a sounding board—is letting her sleep until the friend has to go back to prison in a few weeks for breaking her parole.

All of this unfolds in context to that simple core question: Will Lisa get to remain in this country? Will she find a kidney and save her daughter? Will love survive it all?

Is *your* core dramatic question as compelling? Is it in context to the character's quest, the antagonism, and the stakes? Or is the question smothered in a series of episodic, anecdotal documentaries of "stuff that happens to your hero," included for the misguided purpose of attempting to show us as much of your hero's life and inner self as possible?

If the latter describes your core dramatic question, this may explain the rejection e-mail tacked to your bathroom wall or wherever you keep the rejections that have come your way.

Now you know. And knowing is the key to reversing this trend.

Let's see how much of this has sunk in. As an exercise, beneath the definition of your core dramatic story that you jotted down earlier, write down the core dramatic question. If it's clearer now, more compelling, a win-or-lose proposition relative to a core hero's quest to solve a problem and/or attain a goal, then you are probably on the right track. Bravo to you if that's the case, because this single issue of core story focus, when fumbled, sinks more stories than most authors realize.

The Critical Role of *Stakes*

When you land on a compelling dramatic core story and the dramatic question it poses, you've already defined the stakes. The reader should know, early on, what the consequences of success or failure will be. If you're still only vaguely defining the stakes of your story as "happiness" or "peace" or "to find himself in a cold, cruel world," congratulations—you've just found the probable weakness in your story. Those stakes aren't strong enough, because they are outcomes rather than proactive actions. Good stories are always about the decisions and actions characters choose rather than the exploration of desires and needs the character does not act upon.

Lisa's story quest, in this context, isn't merely to make her daughter healthy and happy. That's the ultimate goal, the point of her quest, the outcome she seeks to attain. The stakes are the "why" of seeking the outcome (consequences of either success or failure), and those stakes attach to the action as much as the goal. This is because the goal *depends* on the action taken—that's where the drama resides. The story needs to be primarily focused on action in a narrative sense. You can't spend four hundred pages writing about what she wants and all that it means, but you *can* spend 390 of those pages writing about *how she engages* with the journey to obtain her goal.

If that's not how you've handled the tradeoff between the hero's goal and the hero's action in your story—with a significant focus on the *journey* that illustrates those actions and confrontations, with the stakes vividly and viscerally established—then you just may have found one of the reasons your manuscript isn't getting the response you hoped for. The fix is at hand, based on your understanding of the actions-in-pursuit-of goals narrative dynamic.

In our example, Lisa's quest and the actions she takes are all about finding her daughter a healthy kidney and a way to get it. The narrative shows that journey, rather than dwelling on the reasons why, because those reasons were vividly implanted in the story back in the Part One setup quartile. This is what she must *do* to save her daughter. A healthy daughter is the desired outcome. The stakes apply to both. But make no mistake, the core story's *dramatic quest* and the *dramatic question* that arises from it are about what she must *do and achieve* to get there. As the author of the story, this is your sweet spot.

The big mistake here would be to dive too deeply inside Lisa's head to simply expose her angst and worry and fear, without including the forward movement of her proactive efforts to solve the problem at hand.

That's a huge story-saving subtlety. It's the difference between a story that works and a story that will disappear in a crowd of other overly character-centric genre stories.

Let's commit your new understanding to paper. Write down the stakes your hero is playing for in your story. Whatever you write is the hero's goal. The success-or-failure proposition of this goal becomes your core dramatic question.

Now, beneath that, write down a summary of what your hero does in pursuit of the goal, the major campaigns and efforts and confrontations she must navigate along the path toward resolving the dramatic question. (Bullet points work well here.)

Hopefully, armed with this new and enlightened awareness of what this means and why it is important, you may have just identified—and perhaps repaired—any weakness in this regard that has been holding the story back.

Dramatic Tension Leading to Resolution

The sum of the core story, the core dramatic question, and the stakes, as well as the conflict they create, expressed as the actions and confrontations that manifest along the path toward the goal, determine the level of dramatic tension in your story. You create a character with need or opportunity. You launch a quest to attain it in the presence of an antagonistic force with something significant at stake, which causes the hero to take action and confront the obstacles. This results in the hero's final crescendo of courage, proactive strength, and cleverness that overcomes the obstacle and resolves the situation.

The hero achieves the goal of her quest as a direct result of her decisions and actions and the outcome of specific confrontations. (Or she doesn't attain her goal, despite all of this. It's your story, and you can end it how you please. But be careful to not betray your reader or the integrity of the story's thematic intentions.)

Things get clearer, if not easier, from here.

When you have a compelling concept that has imbued an engaging premise with something inherently intriguing, something that promises the reader a dramatic, empathetically emotional experience because it meets the criteria for an effective premise ... when you are totally focused on a core dramatic story rather than a character profile or a biographical chronicle ... when that core story asks a juicy dramatic question with vivid and urgent stakes ... when you can define those stakes and they make your skin itch because you can feel their weight ... when all of these elements are clear and ready to fire on all cylinders ... then your work in pinning down the rest of the narrative challenge becomes more focused and accessible. No longer will you be rambling through a forest of episodic randomness driven by inner turmoil, still searching for a core story.

Everything that follows in this chapter assumes you have gained clarity about your core story and that it meets the given criteria. If you aren't there yet, spend some time on your definition of your core concept, its dramatic question, the stakes that hang in the balance, and the specific strategies and actions your hero will take to confront an antagonistic force (villain, threat, or obstacle) standing in his way. Wring as much tension and emotion from this as you can, and change what you must to make sure these bases are covered in a compelling way.

VICARIOUS READER EXPERIENCE

In a cool sort of way—one you should never take for granted, because *you* are responsible for this—a vivid vicarious reading experience is a given in a story that features an empathetic hero's quest with comprehensible, relatable, significant, and urgent stakes and a villain we fear and despise. In other words, vicarious reader experience is directly linked to and dependent on the presence of dramatic tension.

But there's one more narrative ingredient you need to consider and implement to achieve a high level of vicarious experience. It's the stark, detailed, sensual, tactile, provocative, thrilling, scary, sexy, dark, joyous (or whatever it needs to be) *story world* within which all this drama and emotional engagement will transpire.

Sometimes vicarious experience goes a long way to express the success of a novel, perhaps over and above the story itself. Thus, the lack thereof may connect to an explanation for the failure of a story.

VICARIOUS READER EXPERIENCE DEFINED

Ever wonder why *Star Wars* was such an iconic smash hit? The primary answer is *vicarious experience*. As audience members, we got to travel through space, visit other planets, engage with alien life forms, fall in love, and fight evil, all from the comfort of our theater seats. Vicarious experience works in any genre, in any setting, and with any experience. The only criteria is the delivery of a vivid sense of time and place that transports the reader from his world into your story world as viscerally and vividly as possible.

A story world is entirely genre dependent. If your story unfolds in a contemporary city, make that city crackle with gritty, authentic details so the reader feels as if he's just stepped out of a subway tunnel. If it's a real city, use the iconic landmarks and cultural hooks of the place to bring it to life. If your story is set in medieval times, let the reader experience the stench of the horses, the clanking of swords and armor, the whistling of arrows through the dank morning forest air, the sour breath of wheezing innkeepers and drunken kings. Show the blood steaming as it pools on the moist, moss-covered ground during a battle. If your story is set in the future on a vessel headed for a new planet, include the scream of rocket engines and the utter quiet of floating in outer space. Take us there, so that when the fireworks and the fear and the seduction and the intrigue unfold, we are already standing next to the hero, inhaling and smelling and feeling every moment of the adventure.

Readers come to genre stories for just this experience. It is the bread and butter of historical novels, westerns, fantasies, and sci-fi, and even gritty mysteries and thrillers that leverage their settings. Make sure you've thrown open the gates of your story world and delivered the experience they've paid to have.

You have a significant story-fixing opportunity at this point if, in your earlier draft, you'd taken the vicarious reader experience essence for granted and largely abandoned a sense of place in favor of plot exposition. (It's a fine line here; once established, a less-is-more context is best, but make sure the tidbits of place you use are alive with color and vibration.) This lack of detail may be contributing to an overall impression that leads to the dreaded reader response of *It just didn't grab me*. Agents and editors reject stories for a lot less.

Chances are, the issue of vicarious reader experience wasn't mentioned in any rejection or feedback you received. Your inner critic probably didn't notice or comment on it either. Nonetheless, reading is always an emotional engagement, regardless of the intellectual appeal, especially in fiction, and nothing says engagement like *being there*. Vicarious reader experience becomes, in that context, a secret narrative weapon for the writer who understands its value. Let that writer be you.

COMPELLING CHARACTERIZATION

Well, duh, you might be thinking, *of course characterization is important.*

Well over half of the general writing conversation seems to focus on character. But all this noise may have contributed to the problems found in many stories, especially in genre fiction. Literary fiction is all about character, while genre fiction isn't—instead it's about the combination of dramatic tension, conceptual richness, and setting. Character *emerges* from the manner in which the hero, and, to a lesser extent, the secondary characters, engage with the plot itself, in context to the story world you've created.

The story-fixing opportunity succeeds or fails depending on your understanding of this subtlety. Don't for a moment think this means that character isn't a critical base to cover. Quite the opposite. The problem is in mishandling characterization by making it the focus of the story to the detriment of dramatic tension. Mishandling refers to valuing backstory, inner landscape, and outward-facing tics and choices over the catalytic prompts provided by plot.

To perform an acid test on the handling—or mishandling—of characterization, look at the presence of backstory, as well as side trips that don't directly connect to the core story's narrative spine. Two quick case studies from my coaching experience will help clarify what this means.

I was doing a fifteen-minute story review at a conference recently. These types of events force the writer to pitch effectively, thus exposing her highest narrative priority (like character trumping dramatic tension). One of my appointments had a truly killer premise to work with. I asked him when that plot actually kicked in. At what moment does the story transition from the character intro and setup to the first steps of the hero's story (a specific quest, with a clear goal arising from a specific problem and need, and a villain)?

He knew exactly what I was referring to. (It's called the First Plot Point, by the way, which we discuss in chapter eight.) He enthusiastically laid it out for me, and it, too, was nicely crafted.

But he didn't answer my question. I asked it a slightly different way: Where in the story, in terms of a percentage of total pages, does this plot moment occur?

His answer: "It happens somewhere around the midpoint."

And thus his rejection was largely explained.

This is a structural issue, certainly, but one caused by the author overplaying character setup within the structural paradigm, which has a prescribed length for that goal. He spent nearly half of the novel introducing the character, slathering on truckloads of backstory, giving us little vignettes showing the hero playing with his kids, beating down some bad guys during a previous nonrelated case, showing how his boss was an arrogant jerk, even including a scene of the character working out in the weight room to show how jacked he was. The author defended all of these scenes, arguing that each one fleshed out a deep character that the reader would empathize with and root for.

But how he handled it basically killed the story. He had *way* too much character introduction. It was a thriller, and thrillers live and die by their plots, via a provocative dramatic question that defines a core story. When characterization continues beyond the first quartile without that dramatic question being posed, the story is in trouble. By the midpoint (which has its own mission within the story), readers are begging for something to happen, for the story itself to kick in (if they haven't bailed already). They didn't come for the character, especially within the spy genre (which this story was). That's true in any genre story, with the possible exception of literary fiction, and with the particularly complex exception of series novels and films in which the hero is the big draw, like Lee Child's Jack Reacher or James Patterson's Alex Cross. With a series story we return for the character, but that doesn't license an overplayed setup. Indeed, in a series installment we already have met the hero, meaning it is more important than ever to pose a compelling dramatic question early in the narrative. Either way, whether a stand-alone or a series novel, the reader wants to see that hero engaging with a plot, one that certainly doesn't take two hundred pages to finally show up.

I explained to the author I was coaching that this First Plot Point moment ideally occurs at about the 20th percentile mark, and that the pages preceding it should contain plot-related setup elements in addition to the hero intro. This isn't formula—the thing that structure cynics fear and loathe. It's story *physics*. Readers need something specific to root for, and if they wait too long they'll either leave or simply not care as much as they need to. Structure is there for a reason: to optimize the story physics that allow the story to work better.

He quickly understood my criticism—and why he wasn't getting much action with the agents he was pitching at the conference—and he promised to study these principles further. This is what happens when writers create their stories by an instinct that hasn't been schooled in the principles of story physics. They've been told that character is the critical element without grasping the subtlety that a character is best showcased in *context* to a plot that gives that character something dramatic and empathetic to *do*.

The other case study that helps illustrate what can go wrong involves a novel I was hired to analyze in its entirety. This writer had a great opening hook but then kicked into the backstory of the hero, beginning in childhood, and then followed it by dozens of pages that brought the hero up to the present day. Much like the previous example, readers were asked to hit the pause button on the story until this overwrought biography was in place. What this writer did differently, though, was devote the same depth of backstory exposition to every character in the story, even if he or she had no significant role. The guy who delivered a pizza in one scene got four paragraphs of life story and then was never seen again.

That, by the way, is a massive mistake, and a telling one. The writer isn't *there* yet.

Backstory is relevant in genre fiction only to the extent that it explains something about the hero's character as it relates to the unfolding—or soon to unfold—core dramatic story. And it is best given in quick chunks, with artfully nuanced references to the past, something that is much easier to do in first-person narrative than in third.

Structure is driven by the core story. The plot. Character, critical as it is, is woven in and around those structural elements. Stories work best that way. Your rejection, or the need to revise, could very well stem from your well-intended but overplayed emphasis on character over and apart from how it pertains to the plot, specifically to how the hero acts, feels, and responds as she moves along the core dramatic spine toward resolution.

If this sounds like you, one way to refocus your characterization and optimize your story is to revise toward creating a truly three-dimensional character.

Dimensions of Character

Stories are sometimes criticized for being "one-dimensional," which implies there are other dimensions to fully inform your character than the one shown in your pages.

We live in a three-dimensional world. A character can be described in three-dimensional terms as well.

- **FIRST DIMENSION:** This is backstory—the information about where the character came from that helps explain who he is now. In your manuscript, make sure you focus on backstory issues that actually explain how the character engages with the core story rather than resorting to an entire biography. We don't need to hear, for example, about the hero's childhood athletic prowess unless it left a residual scar or precipitated some herculean combat skills that will be used in the core story. Don't mention his abusive mother unless she caused physical or psychological damage that is germane to the narrative.
- **SECOND DIMENSION:** This is how the world views the character in the present story time—the face, and perhaps the mask, the character shows to the world in order to create a desired perception. It's an image that the hero is trying to live up to, a culture into which he is trying to fit. Looks, style, cars, clothes, hobbies, tics, habits, manner of speech … all of these are second-dimensional tools of characterization. Remember: Your goal with characterization has several facets: You want a layered, nuanced character, a complex character, someone we may or may not like but will certainly root for and empathize with relative to the core story. During revision, make your second-dimensional choices with these goals in mind.

- **THIRD DIMENSION:** These are the decisions the character makes under tension, in the face of danger, in the critical moment of action and exposition. This includes his fears and phobias, which may defy his second-dimensional façade. The third dimension is also the playing field of character arc, where we see a hero conquering inner demons and fears using courage and the weight of consequences. Our actions define our true character more than our hairstyles and the cars we drive. Ask O.J. Simpson about this. Ask John Edwards, Anthony Weiner, Jim and Tammy Faye Bakker, Bill Clinton, and hundreds of others who failed to resist temptation and fear under pressure, marring a glistening public façade. Ask Aron Ralston (who severed his own arm to escape a boulder in a canyoneering accident), Dennis Weichel (who sacrificed his life to save a young Afghan girl), New York City police officer Lawrence DePrimo (who gave his shoes to a homeless person in Times Square one freezing night), and countless others who, in a moment of truth, stepped up and revealed who they really are.

These dimensions become tools that allow you to flesh out characters from all angles, giving you more to work with than abusive childhoods and psychologically scarring incidents from the past, even when those backstories apply. It's what the character does going forward, in context to such a backstory, that fleshes out who he has become. An understanding of these three dimensions might even help you see why your characterizations have been judged harshly. Look at how you've cast your hero (especially) and secondary characters in the story you are fixing. See if your emphasis on backstory has taken the urgency and drama away from the core dramatic plot. See if your players are cliché, lacking layers and complexity and nuance. How do all of these things affect the reader's ability to root for and empathize with the hero's quest?

That last question is critical. When we get to the topic of structure in the next chapter, you'll see that the reader's ability to root for and empathize with the hero is one of the primary missions of a four-part, milestone-driven structural flow. It's all about reader response, and character remains one of the most critical, yet tricky, weapons we wield as writers in that regard.

READER EMPATHY

Nearly all the topics we've discussed thus far—a compelling concept and an irresistible premise, dramatic tension, vicarious experience, and resonant characters—exist as tools used for a single desired outcome: to engage the reader in an emotional manner.

This is how fiction differs from nonfiction. The primary mission of nonfiction is to inform, to engage the reader on an intellectual level. Sometimes nonfiction seeks and relies on an emotional component as well, but not with the same fierce singularity as fiction.

READER EMPATHY DEFINED

Reader empathy occurs when the reader feels the hero's pain, fear, and anxiety, or her joy, desire, and anticipation. The reader relates to what the hero is doing, what she wants, her situation and need, the fear or longing for the stakes that are in play. We understand what all that must be like.

Empathy also has a hidden agenda: It increases the likelihood of the reader to root for the hero in the quest or mission you've given her.

There's a flip side to this, too. As writers we want that empathetic fear to cause the reader to despise and root *against* the villain or antagonistic force. To fear him and seek his defeat and demise. An avid fan not only roots for her team to win but also hopes to see the opposing team fail. She cheers when the opposing team fumbles the ball every bit as much as when her team scores or makes a great play.

We generate this "rootability" by manipulating other essences and tools. The degree to which readers relate to a character depends on the degree to which they emotionally engage with the character's story quest. The pace of the exposition, through structure, keeps readers on the edge of their chairs, and our ability to strategically escalate dramatic plot is what deepens the reader's empathy—and the source of their rooting—as the story grows darker and more urgent.

This is why craft is an all-or-nothing proposition in many ways. You can understand all this in theory, but in practice the end effect is determined by how well, how strategically, and how powerfully you have integrated all of these tools and essences within a narrative strategy.

The key question for the story fixer squaring off with a revision is this: How strongly will the reader root for the hero, and why?

This is an imprecise judgment call, to be sure. For example, some people root for Dick Cheney; others are rooting for karma to come full circle on his next hunting trip. The above question is where you place your bet. Your answer isn't in talent or craft; it's in your *sensibility*—though some might make a good case that story sensibility is, in fact, the raw grist of storytelling "talent." Story sensibility is why some authors who follow these principles still don't end up with their pictures in a Barnes & Noble window.

By now it should be apparent that a story that simply chronicles a fictional character's life story, a travelogue of her adventures, and a deep dive into her backstory gives us much to observe, or even to marvel at, but little to *root for*. Even in the presence of empathy, it is possible for your story to be too light on the rootable motivation.

Your story needs a quest, a mission, something for the hero to do. To seek. To avoid. To defeat. To give or to take. The quest must include provocative, weighty stakes that readers can relate to because they understand what they mean, for the hero, for themselves, for anyone.

If your story leans into plot-light character observation but lacks rootability—because the hero is not really doing anything other than living out one anecdotal episode after another—this undercuts the power of the entire narrative, rendering it soft and less than compelling. It will get you rejected.

If you can find this, if you can see it, using the criteria and focuses discussed here, then you can make the changes necessary. These include:

- **INCREASING THE STAKES.** The bigger the win, and the deeper the cut of a loss, the better, because dramatic tension is fueled by stakes.
- **MAKING THE CHARACTER MORE RELATABLE AND EASIER TO EMPATHIZE WITH.** Give your hero some humanity, some temptations and weaknesses, and be sure to show her being a really likeable sort, especially in the Part One setup quartile. Show her stepping up for a friend or a stranger in need, or planning for the future in some way. Show her performing an act of courage and selflessness.
- **MAKING THE VILLAIN MORE HEINOUS.** Depict him as sociopathic, cold-hearted, and even sadistic. Position the villain's intended outcome as inherently selfish. Avoid moustache twirling. The villain at least needs to be less than conflicted about what he's up to, if he's not having a great time doing it.
- **MAKING THE TICKING CLOCK LOUDER AND THE OBSTACLES MORE OMINOUS.** Assign a deadline for what the hero needs to accomplish. Let the reader sense the ticking of that clock by showing how the hero feels and responds to the pressure and anxiety of time running out.

All of these will contribute to dramatic tension and the effect of conflict in the story. If you can isolate these essences and focus on strengthening them in your revision, then your story will have a second life. It will be resurrected.

You can now see how important it is for the writer to fully understand the nature of critical feedback and the places to look for these weaknesses. Defending a story on these issues (i.e., resisting the feedback) can be as much an indicator of naïveté, ignorance, and hubris as it is an injustice.

Feedback is a gift. Developing a story sense that can sniff out these weaknesses is a weapon. Give yourself this gift, arm yourself properly, and watch your story sensibility soar.

THEMATIC WEIGHT

The theme of *The Help* is racial prejudice. It also touches on themes of
class struggles, cultural influence, and sexism.

The theme of *Gone Girl* is the treacherous landscape of marriage,
pure and simple. Marriage is hard. Sometimes it's dark and horrible.
Psychotic people have a hard time with marriage. That's what the book
asks us to think about.

Nelson DeMille's fabulous novel *Up Country* takes his war veteran
hero back to Vietnam thirty years later to investigate a crime for the
U.S. government. It has themes on the cruelty of war and the impro-
priety of the Vietnam War in particular, midlife career crisis, love and
family, and forgiveness. This is an example of a theme virtually writing
itself. You simply can't write about Vietnam without the cruelties and
inequities of that theater bubbling up through the narrative.

Notice how those themes cut across several categories. Things that
happen. The nature of entities and cultures and people. The scope of

a moral compass. The issue isn't what your theme is. Frankly, themes will emerge from a story without any effort whatsoever on your part. If you have characters who exist in the world, who interact and live within microcosms (cultures, societies, and organizations), all with certain assumptions, settings, and parameters, then theme happens. It will be there.

This is often the case in deep genre stories. They unfold according to the tropes of the genre—romance is a great example—without any effort whatsoever on the author's part to *say something* thematic in the narrative. "Love is hard," even "love sucks," will be a hard message to avoid in a love story, because, as in any genre, the nuclear core source of energy in a romance is conflict. And conflict is almost always thematic.

Then again, there are stories where the theme is intentional—the story has an agenda, a point of view to sell you. The novels of Jodi Picoult are a case in point. She's created an entire cottage industry by fictionalizing recent events and going deep to examine the sociological and psychological genesis of what led to these events.

In her 2008 novel *Nineteen Minutes*, we meet the two young perpetrators who would end up shooting and killing nine students and one teacher at Columbine High School in Colorado. The thematic question was never the right or wrong of their actions but rather the social pressures and cruelties perpetrated upon those boys, and the response by parents, teachers, and the various institutions that define that sociology. Dramatic tension was never the engine here, since we all know how the tragic events of the shooting unfolded. And Picoult never needs to comment on the equity of those episodes from the past, as this approach is one of the few that licenses episodic narrative, which in this case is in context to the unfolding of a too-familiar present day plot. She simply hits the "play" button and allows the horror to rain down upon us, firing the furnace of our own outrage and allowing us to sublimate it all into our own life experiences. There isn't a moment of preaching or journalistic documentary anywhere within her story.

Pulling that off, of course, is pure art ... the art of thematic writing at its finest.

Theme may or may not have been a factor in the rejection of your story. If you are writing within a deep genre—mystery, romance, fantasy, or science fiction—odds are that it wasn't a factor. Other niches, however—literary fiction, historical fiction, adult contemporary—are richest when readers are immersed in a thematic context that allows them to feel the same pressures as the characters.

When theme surfaces as a deal breaker, it is usually because the writer tried *too* hard to sell a polarizing and controversial point of view, to recruit readers to one side or another. When overselling theme trumps logic and dramatic effectiveness, it'll get you tossed.

In a story I coached, the author had his hero gun down senators who didn't align with the author's political beliefs and then had the Supreme Court pardon the killer because, darn it, those senators deserved to die.

Theme can kill you, too, if you're too transparent.

Look at the themes in your story. Is there a particular theme about which you feel strongly? Something you care deeply about and hoped to make a statement about for your readers? If you're writing about love or politics or religion or other aspects of human existence, then your story probably contains more themes than you even know. If you're trying to rewrite history, or if you're messing with laws of nature or predicting future agendas, then you need to be conscious of what you're doing in terms of manipulating the reader toward a specific point of view. Dan Brown walked the line in *The Da Vinci Code*, but it worked in his favor: Of the 80 million people who bought the book, a massive percentage were angry and resentful of how Brown challenged their personal belief systems. No doubt there were those who bought the book just to see why everyone was so upset, but that's certainly not the optimal narrative strategy for any story. Getting the reader emotionally engaged is always the smarter bet.

Make that choice at your own peril. It's a fine line.

8
NARRATIVE BODYBUILDING
PART TWO

STORY ARCHITECTURE

By definition, stories unfold in a certain order. Publishable ones, that is. Therefore, we can conclude that if a story is unpublishable, it's likely because it *lacks* that certain order.

That order is known as *structure*. For some, it's the most terrifying word in all of fiction. For others—especially those who cast off old, limiting beliefs—it can be the salvation of a story.

Every story has structure, for better or worse. Its presence is never in question—only its effectiveness, clarity, and power. To leave those critical variables to chance, or at the mercy of your own sensibilities, is like trying to do brain surgery on a hunch, when proven science is available to ensure that the patient lives to see another day.

STORY STRUCTURE DEFINED

Story structure, which is a subset of "story architecture," is the order in which narrative exposition unfolds. The classic form of story structure shows a story unfolding in three "acts"—a setup, confrontation, and resolution. Some story gurus and analysts expand that model to provide a deeper contextual definition, but nearly every viable model begins with or is drawn from the three-act structure. All structures arise from an intuitive flow that consists of a beginning, a middle, and an end, and all of these structures attempt to assign meaning and context to all three (or more) of those sequential segments.

"Story architecture," on the other hand, is the integration of sequential structure with the more aesthetic elements of character arc, dramatic tension, and reader engagement, the sum of which constitutes the full presentation of the story to its reader. This analogous term arises from architecture itself as the core essence of the design and construction of buildings. It is no accident that the word *building* is synonymous with the word *structure*, which are interchangeable terms for describing a house or a large dwelling. Architecture includes the shapes and artful blending of materials, colors, and images that attach to the core structure itself.

Writers fall into three categories where structure is concerned.

1. Organic Writers

These writers unspool their stories organically, completely relying on their current level of intuitive story sensibility (for some, this manifests as guesswork), which is often informed by their experience as readers of stories and viewers of films. They may never have heard of or glimpsed a story structure model or paradigm before. If you're in this camp, you get a sense of how stories unfold and what goes where by reading novels and seeing movies, and then following your gut to allow the story to unfold as it spills from your mind through a keyboard or pen onto the page.

As I've said before, this is a common, if risky, way to work. It's like thinking you can repair a toilet because you've been sitting on one for all these years—many have discovered the folly of following that hunch. Sometimes the author's sense of structure works as a guiding instinct, but more often it's problematic, resulting in a complete mess.

That writer from the earlier example with the First Plot Point squarely in the middle of his draft? He was in this category. He was organic, and lost. While his premise was strong, his sensibility ultimately failed him.

2. Structural Story Designers

These are writers who understand and abide by certain principles of story structure, most of which are built upon and around that three-act dramatic paradigm. Screenwriters in particular live and die by this model, to the extent that script readers will reject a work if the First Plot Point hasn't shown up by page 30. What's interesting about this approach is that the structure of a story that works, that will find an agent and/or a publisher and ultimately attract readers, is the *exact same one* for organic writers and structural story designers. The same structural flow—setup, confrontation, resolution, however you break it down into even more finite and clearly defined parts—is what any story will look like … when it works.

The criteria for structure is the same—exactly the same—for organic writers and for those who design their stories. Which means that organic writers, using multiple drafts driven by feedback and their own state of story sensibility, are moving toward that form and function from square one, molding their story toward that end format. Story designers begin with the format and install their unfolding story into it.

The difference is one of *process*, not outcome. In a published book (at least a traditionally published book, as improperly structured self-published books do find their way into the market), nothing other than the author's knowledge of structure, which may or may not be informed, vets the story.

There are many versions of this principle, mine included, circulating within the writing conversation. But upon close examination they are all closely aligned with a basic flow and architecture. All of them send the story to the very same structural destination. Some models break that structure down into more concise subsets with four or more acts. Don't be fooled, though—the contextual flow of the story is the same across most of these models.

Writers in this camp follow these structures because they make sense to them, they work, and they are evident in successfully published works and produced films. Structure isn't something you invent but rather something you can interpret and apply to your own premise and character needs.

3. Deniers

Finally, there are some who reject the notion of structure altogether. These writers, though fully aware of viable structural models, advocate allowing the story to spill out of their heads onto the page and trusting their story senses to optimize the outcome. If this sounds like the organic writer's process, that's accurate ... but only through the first couple of drafts. Enlightened organic writers—and there are many, some you've heard of (Stephen King, Diana Gabaldon, Jeffery Deaver, and so on)—know the story isn't done until it aligns with the principle-modeled flow of structure, even if they refuse to call it by that name. Deniers—those who don't know or reject the principles of structure—label their drafts final when it suits them, sometimes with major structural flaws still glaringly in place.

I see this all the time in my coaching work; it's one of the most common sources of story weakness and failure. Perhaps you already see yourself in one of these three categories and already sense that the way your story unfolds structurally is where it took a dive.

The denial method is confusing and paradoxical on several counts.

First, those who use it are actually preaching about a preference of *process* rather than an alternate structural format for a finished, polished story—even though, in their defense of process, they are saying the opposite by declaring structure is formulaic. (There are many formats, but upon closer examination you'll see that the variance is a degree of depth; all viable forms have the three- or four-act structure as its basis.) This is a naïve and inaccurate perception, by the way (if you doubt this, use the classic structural paradigm and test it against best-selling novels and produced films; you'll see it in action every time). Spilling words from their heads onto the page is their preferred method of searching for their story. It's how they get their premise on paper. And because many of these nonbelievers (some of whom believe the characters are telling them what to do or that they are getting guidance from some cloud-dwelling muse with a knack for fiction) have experience and some degree of story sense, it turns out well for them.

Don't be fooled by these writers. As I said, their successful stories almost always end up aligning with the very architectural models they reject.

The first goal of revising your story's structure is to understand which of these three groups you fall within.

Your story bears witness to this, but don't look there to find out. Rather, go back to your process and acknowledge what structural context you used or rejected. If you didn't align with a proven model, or if you drank the Kool-Aid and simply wrote what you felt in the moment, chances are that this is the number-one reason why your story didn't work as well as intended. Your revision work will focus on bringing your story flow into a keen alignment with the principles of story structure.

This circles back to an earlier point. There are two categories of story failure: The story isn't good enough, or the execution wasn't up to snuff. Messing with, ignoring, or being ignorant of basic story structure principles easily transforms great premises into defective manuscripts.

Chances are high that your revision will focus right here, at the structural level.

Find another process.

This is *revision*. It's no longer about what seemed fun, what felt good, or what Stephen King says. You're in a pit here, one into which King has likely never fallen, and you need to dig your way out of it. Story structure, as defined by proven principles that millions of novels and screenplays have adhered to (most very rigorously) may be your best hope and your strongest tool to fix it. My advice, culled from coaching hundreds of clients who have sent me structurally broken stories, is this: Learn the model. Call it three-act structure or four-part narrative flow (my preference), but they are essentially the same thing.

The model I teach and apply for story analysis defines a flow of four different contexts—the mission of that quartile of your narrative—across the entire arc of the story. This actually shows you what to write and where to put it. When you have determined your core story, this model is deliriously liberating. You are shown what level of exposition and transparency to apply to specific parts of the story, as well as what each transitional milestone needs to accomplish and where it should appear. (A transitional milestone is a scene or a single moment within a scene when the whole story changes, such as when the ship hits the iceberg in the movie *Titanic*.)

Here is what that four-part structure looks like when presented graphically:

BASIC STORY STRUCTURE

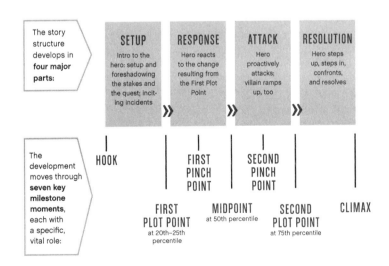

Many writers have told me that the understanding and adoption of this as a story-flow paradigm, as a guideline through the maze of story options, as a means of helping decide what to write and where to put it, is the single most empowering thing they've ever experienced in their writing journey. They sometimes tell me this after decades of wandering around in a forest of less concise options, one of which is to pay no attention to structure at all.

To help you navigate this four-part flow by adding specific context-driven missions that fall within them, see the chart on the next several pages, which lists the various story models endorsed by some of today's most well-known story teachers and gurus. Noted screenwriting guru Art Holcomb provided this list, and it's an invaluable tool. Note how none of these writing mentors is in disagreement. Rather, any differences here are matters of specificity and degree.

I have written hundreds of pages about this model, both in my two previous writing books and on my website. *Story Engineering* (my first writing book) delivers a deep dive into this model, defining and exploring the meanings of the terms and the missions of the elements, and both *Story Engineering* and *Story Physics* offer examples from bestsellers that show this model in spectacularly effective execution. Rather than repeat that content here, I direct you to these books and many others, including the iconic *Screenplay: The Foundations of Screenwriting* by Syd Field. These titles will help you internalize this story-saving, life-giving theory and model.

For now, though, these graphics say it all.

If this was a war, you would have just been given a Sherman tank. Or an F-18, which is a more apt analogy. The solution to your revision challenge is right in front of you.

A cynic might ask how issues relative to concept, character, theme, or a flat writing voice can be observed and fixed using a structural model. That's a fair question.

Scene execution and writing voice, which are two of the six core competencies, can't be improved from this structural perspective. Scene placement, however, is totally driven by structure. A structure model allows you to examine your existing scenes to see if they align

3 STEPS (TRADITIONAL)

Beginning

Middle

End

5 STEPS (MCKEE)

Inciting Incident

Progressive Complications

Crisis

Climax

Resolution

5 STEPS (SEGER)

Setup

First Turning Point

Second Turning Point

Climax

Resolution

5 STEPS (HAUGE)

Turning Point 1: Opportunity

Turning Point 2: Change
of Plans

Turning Point 3: Point
of No Return

Turning Point 4: Major
Setback

Turning Point 5: Climax

7 STEPS (FIELD)

Inciting Incident

Plot Point 1

Pinch 1

Midpoint

Pinch 2

Plot Point 2

Climax

8 STEPS (DANIEL)

Status Quo (II)

Predicament Lock-In

First Obstacle (Raising Stakes)

First Culmination (Midpoint)

Subplot (Rising Action)

Main Culmination (End of Act 2)

New Tension (Twist)

Resolution

14 STEPS (BELL)

The Disturbance

The Care Package

The Argument Against Transformation

Trouble Brewing

Doorway to No Return 1

A Kick in the Shins

The Mirror Moment

Pet the Dog

Doorway to No Return 2

Mounting Forces

Lights Out

The Q Factor

Final Battle

Transformation

15 STEPS (SNYDER)

Opening Image

Setup

Theme Stated

Catalyst

Debate

Break into Act 2

B Story

Promise of the Premise

Midpoint

Bad Guys Close In

All Is Lost

Dark Night of the Soul

Break into Act 3

Finale

Final Image

22 STEPS (TRUBY)

Self Revelation (Need/Desire)

Ghost and Story World

Weakness and Need

Inciting Incident

Desire

Ally or Allies

Opponent and/or Mystery

Fake-Ally Opponent

First Revelation/Decision, Change Desire/Motive

Plan

Opponent's Plan/Main Counterattack

Drive

Attack by Ally

Apparent Defeat

Second Revelation/Decision: Obsessive Drive, Changed Desire/Motive

Audience Revelation

Third Revelation and Decision

Gate, Gauntlet, Visit to Death

Battle

Self-Revelation

Moral Decision

New Equilibrium

17 STEPS (CAMPBELL)

Call to Adventure

Refusal of the Call

Supernatural Aid

Crossing First Threshold

Belly of the Whale

Road of Trials

Meeting with Goddess

Woman as Temptress

Atonement with Father

Apotheosis

Ultimate Boon

Refusal of Return

Magic Flight

Rescue from Without

Crossing Return Threshold

Master of Two Worlds

Freedom to Live

18 STEPS (BROOKS)

Hook

Character Intro and Positioning

Foreshadowing, Intro of Stakes and Threat, Intertwined with Setup

Mechanism of FPP Turn

First Plot Point, Core Story Launch

Hero Responds and Heads Down New Path

Threat Lurks, Builds, or Evolves

Midpoint Context Shift (New Info)

Hero Changes Course

Antagonist Ups the Game, Stakes Increase

Trial and Error, Confrontation

Lull (Hope Seems Lost)

Second Plot Point Story Shift

Hero Becomes More Heroic and Clever

Truth Emerges and/or Changes

Final Confrontation Moment

Resolution

How the World Returns to New Normal

with the optimal context assigned to them. Scenes that have the wrong content and context, or are located in the wrong place within the structure, are some of the most common story toxins you can name, so don't take this lightly.

Theme is more about a perception of the whole story, so structure isn't the right tool for strengthening it. That said, a story that works—and structure *is* the right tool for achieving that—is the best place within which to empower a theme, so adjust your cynicism accordingly.

Can this model improve your concept and your premise?

Absolutely it can. The highest calling of concept and premise is the degree to which it lends itself to dramatic tension and character arc, how it creates a landscape for each of the physics of storytelling to work its magic.

The same is true for many of the other elements. Pacing is completely driven by this structural model. Optimal pacing calls for certain expositional content that escalates a story to appear in specific places proven to be the ideal location relative to the reading experience. This model doesn't allow for a slow opening, or for focusing on one essential structural context to the detriment of another, which is what happens, for example, when the opening setup quartile is short-changed in the impatience to fully launch the core story (which happens at the First Plot Point milestone, at the intersection of Part One and Part Two with the model). Pacing and structure go hand in hand, generating twists and changing the story in major ways at the right spots, yet leaving you free to insert other surprises as you see fit.

Such narrative surprises (often called *plot twists*), in turn, empower the reading experience relative to character empathy and the vicarious experience. They make the story more vivid, more fluid. If the premise isn't boring, execution along this model ensures that the reader won't be bored in the telling.

A Structure for Character

Like a medicine for, say, hair loss that also causes you to lose weight, this four-part narrative flow facilitates an optimally succinct character arc as well. This was first observed in 1989 in a book by Carol S. Pearson, which contains an expanded version of this model in its title: *Six Archetypes We Live By: Innocent, Orphan, Magician, Wanderer, Martyr, Warrior.*

I know, that's six. But all of these fit into one of the four parts in our storytelling structure. Part One, for example, is called the Setup because it inserts all the preliminary context and elements necessary to unleash the plot and—notice this—our empathy for the hero. In the context of character, this quartile is labeled the Orphan stage (thus also embracing the Innocent stage), which begins with a hero who is innocent relative to the journey she is about to take, in effect "orphaned" from a core story that has yet to emerge and engage.

Here are those four character labels aligned with the four expositional parts of the flow:

EXPOSITION/PLOT	CHARACTER/ARC
Part 1: Setup	Innocent/Orphan
Part 2: Response	Wanderer/Magician
Part 3: Attack	Warrior
Part 4: Resolution	Martyr/Hero

The affinity between these contexts—plot exposition and character arc—becomes the key to the narrative kingdom for writers seeking to understand the best way to tell their stories. And for those who look away and choose to rely on their instincts, the draft that finally works—likely after several revisions—will still look very much like the table shown above.

You did it your way in your draft, for whatever reason. Now it has been judged as deficient; it was denied access to the next step. It's on you to fix that. To repair the narrative. Chances are the solution is right here, in the structural realm. Now you know where to look. And with a deeper embrace of the principles of story architecture, you know how to strengthen it as well.

OPTIMAL PACING

The good thing about pacing, in context to the format of structure, is that you are still encouraged, perhaps driven, by your now-evolved story sense to add your own bells and whistles within this structural paradigm. To make the story your own, dress it up as you please within this framework.

An athlete has a field of play and lines that define the sport. All she is tasked with is to play the game within those lines. The same goes for the writer. Within those parameters, you can move any way you want: Dance a jig, do somersaults, bob and weave and cut and feint and push and mow someone down, be coy or go for the throat, play big or play small, crawl or run or do whatever your game plan and your instincts tell you to do. When someone suggests the structural model is nothing other than a formula, think of this analogy. You have infinite freedom to improvise within the lines.

Formula is not necessarily a bad word. Genre fiction, by definition, places formulaic expectations right in front of you. How you create between those lines of expectation dictates your level of art.

Without those lines you have a gang fight or a riot or finger-painting that slops off the canvas.

Pace is one of the best beneficiaries of structure, by whatever process you apply it. Organic, design, or denial, plan or no plan, outline or draft—however you search for and develop your story—when the manuscript needs to stand alone and your process no longer matters, the model applies. It is there for you, ready to guide you, waiting to rescue you.

Remember that example I gave you earlier about the writer whose novel was devoted to character intro and setup in the first half? Now you can see how it was a structural disaster, a deal-killing outcome of his process. But perhaps now you can also see that the specific reason it's a deal killer is that the story's pace was compromised. Destroyed, actually. Pacing, or lack thereof, killed the story. He needed to reframe his story within the structural paradigm—compress the setup into the first quartile, leading toward a killer First Plot Point moment that shifts the context of everything from setup into a fully ignited, dramatic core plot. In hindsight, the fix is obvious.

SCENE EXECUTION

At some point in the writing process, the rubber must meet the road. Narrative happens. Whether in outline or draft, the most critical step of all is beginning to write actual expositional scenes.

SCENE EXECUTION DEFINED

Scenes are stand-alone units of exposition. There are many kinds of scenes, some introductory, some transitional, some of them major story milestones, the stuff of movie trailers.

Most novels have between forty and sixty scenes, and some have many more. The novels of James Patterson, for example, often have well over one hundred scenes, presented as discrete chapters. That said, a "chapter" may or may not be a single scene, and, conversely, a single scene may or may not be a full chapter. There is no guideline on this; your story sensibility makes that call. You can put as many scenes into a chapter as you choose, but do so in a way that

Scenes become the intersection of intention and execution, of vision
and outcome. Right here is where greatness materializes, or where the
story becomes *less than*. This is where you actually *write*. Because even
if a premise glows in the dark and the characters are memorable and
moving, scenes are the stage upon which they are presented. And if the
lighting is off and the direction and choreography of the scene don't
work, the story is compromised or deflates entirely.

The trouble is, some authors simply don't write their scenes well
enough. This manifests in two ways: (1) Their scenes don't work as they
should, because the flow is awkward—it takes too long to put the intention of the scene into play—or (2) their sentences and styling are not at
a professional level. We'll talk about writing voice in the next section,
but for now let's examine your scenes to see if this is where your novel
or screenplay shot itself in the foot.

Every scene needs a *mission*.

This might be the single most relevant pointer in all of fiction writing.
Read it again: *Every scene needs a mission*. A specific function and purpose, relative to what expositional information it imparts to the story.
Every scene should contribute something relative to exposition, which
may include a new twist on something already in play. (A twist, by definition, is something *changing* within the story). The mission is rarely to
focus *only* on character (you can get away with a few—and only a few—
of these scenes, especially in the Part One setup quartile) but rather to *illustrate* character as plot exposition and flow take place within the scene.

Without a scene mission that forwards the story's exposition, the
scene risks becoming filler. Or a side trip. Or a flashback. Everything
stops while such a scene plays out, which is never a good thing.

Another helpful scene-writing tip (with a nod to my colleague
Donald Maass, who is an enthusiastic spokesperson for this one) is the
creation of *microtension* within key individual scenes. Think of the
scene as a one-act play that appears within the contextual flow of the

whole. This scene asks a specific dramatic question. A need or a goal or a problem is in play, and something opposes the hero's actions within the scene. That micro-confrontation is resolved to some degree (which doesn't mean it is completely solved; it merely establishes or escalates a source of tension or other required narrative exposition) in a fashion that moves the whole story forward, to the next step of macro-exposition.

Any scene that is not in context to an efficient core story spine, created in context to where it appears within the four context-defining quartiles of structure, and in context to an ending that awaits and requires foreshadowing and nuanced setup, will risk being aimless, even chaotic, if not outright irrelevant.

How Scenes Go South

Writing effective scenes is challenging to teach. This is truly a sensibility issue, one that improves with practice and in noticing how scenes flow within the work of published novels and produced movies. This is always most effective when such observation is informed by a familiarity with these principles. If your scenes feel and read differently than the mission-driven criteria demands, if you are using scenes primarily (or solely) to create your own unique prose footprint, you may be at risk. This may be where the need for revision will be most obvious.

Revising for optimal scene execution requires you to examine each scene and perceive if it contains any of the following weaknesses. Take your time, and regard each scene as a stand-alone piece of work, almost as a story in its own right.

- **THE SCENE IS NOT CONNECTED TO THE SPINE OF THE CORE DRAMATIC STORY.** It becomes a side trip or an overwrought flashback. (Flashbacks can and should be part of the core story sequence, but only so far as they inform the foreground story rather than display an unconnected or overplayed episode from the past for the sole purpose of characterization, which only works well within the first quartile.)

- **THE SCENE DOES NOT CONTRIBUTE TO THE FORWARD MOMENTUM OF THE STORY.** The pause button has been hit, and the scene seems to linger, to flesh out sideline details or backstory.
- **THE SCENE DOESN'T CUT INTO THE HEART OF ITS TRUE PURPOSE.** Instead it ramps up with descriptions of setting, chitchat between characters, and other nonessential narrative. William Goldman advises us to enter our scenes at the last possible moment and shed the nonessential details that happen *before* the most crucial point. Doing so will force you to understand the mission of the scene and will increase pacing and hold your readers in the tight grip of dramatic tension. If you realize you are writing a scene without a clear mission in mind, if you are searching for a place for the scene to land, then you are in risky territory.
- **THE SCENE IS OUT OF SYNC WITH THE CONTEXT OF THE QUARTILE IN WHICH IT APPEARS.** The beauty of the story structure model is that it assigns four very separate contexts to the scenes within them:

  - **SETUP**—wherein we meet the hero, establish the setting and stakes, and create a path toward the First Plot Point moment.
  - **RESPONSE**—to the launch of the quest, via the First Plot Point.
  - **ATTACK**—based on new information imparted at the midpoint.
  - **RESOLUTION**—wherein the hero becomes the primary catalyst in the quest toward a goal, however that concludes.

    If you are writing Setup scenes beyond the first setup quartile, you are compromising dramatic tension. If you are writing Resolution scenes in the third quartile, you are shortchanging your ending.

- **THE SCENE IS SETTING THE WRONG EXPECTATIONS.** There are many types and categories of scenes, meaning all scenes need to align with the expectations of their designated function. Transitional scenes need to change the story, often in terms of setting, time, and point of view. Introductory scenes, especially in the Setup, have a different mission than action scenes. Then there are key structural milestone scenes (the First Plot Point scene being perhaps the most important scene in the entire story), where the narrative depends on the rendering of a specific dramatic moment. Make sure your story utilizes all of these flavors of scenes, and that they do their job rather than trying to be something they are not. Many revision opportunities may present themselves from this advanced subtlety alone.

If your story sensibility is solid, chances are you're on firm ground with regard to your scenes. You will intuitively place your scenes where they should contextually appear (using the four-part model as a guideline), and when *that* happens you'll notice that you've implemented the story model, even if you don't want to admit this to your pantser writing friends. Otherwise you're at risk of having a story without an optimal flow.

How is your story sensibility at this point? I'm betting it's better than when you wrote the draft you are trying to fix. Keep going—the more you work with these principles, the more they become second nature.

WRITING VOICE

In the end, the task of writing a story boils down to simply writing sentences, all of them appearing within scenes. Not amazing sentences—those are best kept to a brilliantly placed minimum. And not poetic sentences—opt for brilliant irony and transparency over dazzling alliteration.

So far we've been discussing the content of those sentences, as well as their context. In other words, how they contribute to the entirety of exposition. How they connect to what came before, and how they transition to what comes after.

Writers often come to the avocation of storytelling precisely because they believe that they write excellent sentences. Often they are right. They can indeed produce glowing strings of intricate beauty and render piercing truth with vivid imagery.

And sometimes that very belief is what gets them in hot water.

WRITING VOICE DEFINED

Voice is the outcome—the effect on a reader—elicited by the words you choose and the sentences you assemble using them. Voice is your style. It is often unique but sometimes generic in nature. The highest goal of voice is clarity, to not write sentences that call undue attention to themselves in the absence of expositional value. Sometimes voice adds the perfect nuance to your expositional content. "Less is more" is a useful touchstone, since overwriting is easily noticed and never appreciated. Bad prose, unduly distracting prose, rendered in an effort to imbue the narrative with emotion and texture (known as purple prose) has been the cause of many a rejected manuscript.

Issues with Voice

It's obvious why less-than-clean writing will get you rejected: It simply isn't at a professional level when it absolutely must be. What causes this lack of professionalism is less clear; it's easier to identify writing that is not professional than to define what the professional level is. In general, though, you need to cull the weeds from your narrative so that what remains is a clean, smooth, and inviting landscape of words. As a rule, unprofessional writing is often the result of the author trying too hard, putting too much into the sentences in an effort to be colorful, ironic, or clever. The prose becomes *purple* instead of colorful. Less is usually more when it comes to solid writing.

How do we fix writing voice? It involves an investment of time rather than studying a manual. It's voice, and therefore it's a sensibility. It's like telling someone she needs to sing better or to look less clumsy when she walks. The best strategy is to begin noticing how your writing voice compares to the voice of published, successful authors you admire. Try to categorize their voices and observe how they use language. If you can't see the difference between their sentences and yours, then this road will be a long one. If you can, then three words apply:

Practice. Practice. Practice.

And then get feedback. Find someone who cares enough about you to be honest and is also qualified to differentiate between a professional and an amateur writing voice.

In addition to overwriting (purple prose), the writer may be guilty of being clumsy. Perhaps the story is void of whimsy, or the sentences don't create a rhythm or betray the author's lack of experience by coming off as sophomoric. Again, this is an *ear* thing, a sensibility thing. It is something that can be learned over time. Revising your draft for voice boils down to this: Do the best you can with it. Get feedback on the line level rather than just at the story level. Remember that *less is more*. Have someone mark up the pages, focusing on sentences that aren't strong enough. Get help making them better. Create a crash course in evolving your voice as part of your revision, if someone has told you this is the problem.

You don't have to write like Joyce Carol Oates or John Updike to get published. Indeed, the perhaps subconscious attempt to sound like an author you admire can be the source of awkwardness, rendered ironic if you actually succeed in mimicking the author. More writers than you can count have parroted the voice of John Steinbeck, and there isn't a professional editor out there who, upon noticing, will consider it a good thing.

Incidentally, issues of voice might be the only item of feedback you receive from agents and editors. These folks aren't shy about offering their opinions on voice because they don't have to explain it. "Well, it just didn't work for me" or another vague comment might be all that you get from them where voice is concerned.

Dialogue Speaks for Itself

Writing dialogue is its own art form. Even writers who have a smooth narrative voice occasionally write dialogue that sounds like something from a middle school play.

Match dialogue with the nature and worldview of the character speaking it. If the character is really smart, give him layered, sophisticated dialogue, which is not necessarily overly eloquent dialogue. Don't try too hard, as doing so implies bluster rather than intelligence. If the character isn't so bright, reflect this in how he speaks.

There are many tools to help imbue your dialogue with personality. Humor and sarcasm are a few of the most common flavors within dialogue. Also consider the length of dialogue, line by line: Some people speak in short bullets, and others meander through a conversation. Dialect, too, can inform the cultural background of a character and inject personality at the same time.

Here are two versions of the same fictional dialogue. The first sounds like something a grade-school teacher would write in a children's book, while the second is imbued with a casual street sensibility.

THE BAD

"Hi, Steve, how are you doing?"

"Good. And you?"

"Fine, thanks. It has been a while since we've run into each other."

"It has. It's been too long. We should have lunch sometime."

A BETTER VERSION

"Hey, Steve, what's up with you?"

"It's all good. You?"

"Dude, still livin' the dream, man, livin' the dream. It's been too long."

"True that. We should grab a bite, catch up."

Both versions portray character. The first version shows two people without the slightest hint of personality (and if that is your intent, write it that way). But people in the real world just don't talk this way. In the second version, these speakers land squarely in an easily perceived demographic. The point of either isn't to make the reader like them or relate to them but to create a context for the exchange that lends meaning beyond the words they use. In that second version you can almost see the skateboard tucked under the arm of one guy and the backpack slung across the shoulder of the other. Two women greeting each other at the country club would sound quite different, as would two guys in suits running into each other outside of a courtroom.

Rules of grammar, including writing in complete sentences and using *on-the-nose* wording, go out the window when writing dialogue. The rule of thumb is simple: Write dialogue to reflect how real people speak, and customize it to who your character is, where he comes from culturally, and his state of mind as he speaks.

Once again, this is totally a sensibility issue. The same solutions apply: Get feedback, study dialogue from authors with credibility, and practice, practice, practice.

Then ... repeat.

That's how you fix your writing voice. How long that process takes is on you. Here's hoping it clicks once you head down that path. If that voice doesn't add value, or, worse, if it detracts by being too on-the-nose and flat, your good story might just get sent back to you for this reason alone.

The fix is to evolve your dialogue ear. Try to imagine specific people in your life, or even celebrities, who align with the character being written, and hear the dialogue coming from their mouths. Clint Eastwood is likely to say something in a completely different way than LeBron James, even if the meaning of their words is exactly the same.

NARRATIVE STRATEGY

It can be easy to assume that you've automatically adopted the best way to write your book. Often you come to this decision based on your comfort level with a certain approach or style, or maybe you remember your high school composition teacher advising you to never write in first person.

Times have changed. The narrative playing field is wide open. You have choices that can make your story better by virtue of a deeper dive into character and an edgier context for dramatic tension.

NARRATIVE STRATEGY DEFINED

Your narrative strategy is how you choose to render voice, tense, and point of view. It also addresses issues of chapterization, dialogue, and even the use of italics and punctuation. It is the narrative form of the novel, chosen from or perhaps blending a short list of options in that regard.

What used to be the default approach in point of view (third-person omniscient) and tense (past) is being challenged by a highly effective wave of first-person hero narrators and present-tense exposition, which until not long ago were the sole province of screenplays.

Alice Sebold's *The Lovely Bones* was written in first-person present tense from the point of view of a murdered fourteen-year-old girl speaking directly to the reader … *from heaven.* That was not only the narrative strategy, and a whopper of an original one, but it also constituted the concept of the novel, which served to easily differentiate it from other stories in the mystery genre.

The first time I read a book that toggled between first-person hero-narrated chapters and third-person behind-the-curtain point of view from the villain—and yes, you absolutely *can* do that—I thought I'd been transported to another dimension. This particular book was by Nelson DeMille (*The Lion's Game*), and I liked the approach so much that I've written my last two novels in this way. I'm also seeing it used in novels from all genres to great effect.

It isn't just a choice—it's a *strategic* call.

Does the interior monologue inside the head of your hero scream to be heard? If not, making the character more accessible may be a great strategy for revision. First person might have been your best approach—and it's available again now, as you revise—because it creates more intimacy between the protagonist and the reader and allows for the inclusion of seamless backstory as the hero relates present-day moments via thoughts of past experiences.

If you're looking to really shake up the narrative perspective in your story, consider this: Your first-person narrator doesn't have to be the hero at all. *The Great Gatsby,* for example, is narrated by Gatsby's neighbor, Nick Carraway, played by Tobey Maguire in the recent film starring Leonardo DiCaprio as Gatsby. The choice is a strategic one—both for F. Scott Fitzgerald and for you—and could be the means for taking what is perceived to be a vanilla draft to a higher level, something dripping with taste and color.

How do you make this call?

Let the story physics be your guide. If your comfort level turns you away from a choice, realize you may be doing your story a disservice. It's actually easier for you to ramp up your skills in a particular tense or point of view than it is to make up for the sacrifice of tension and intimacy afforded by the options available. Because you've already written the story, revision is the ideal place to test a strategy. The first line of perception is your own story sensibility, but if you can find trusted readers to help you assess a new approach as a revision strategy, be assured they will notice these devices right away.

Look at your story and look at the feedback. Maybe something will click that moves another tense, another point of view, another mixture of modes to the head of the line of candidates for your narrative strategy. If you have been told that your hero is too flat and/or difficult to relate to, consider a rewrite in first person. That alone might bring your hero closer to the reader and thus solve your problem.

AN INVITATION TO DETERMINE WHAT HAS SUNK IN

You are cordially invited to return to those twelve grading points from chapter three and take another pass at evaluating them. Maybe some of those As and Bs are, in reality, and in context to all you've learned, more aptly graded at the C level. And maybe a few low grades are actually stronger than you thought.

To make this exercise even richer, if you've already devised some better story points and execution strategies, plug them into your story and *then* reassess your novel or screenplay against these benchmarks. Grade the story you now intend to write, as the product of a revision, instead of the one that someone else didn't think passed the test.

Doing so will prove the veracity of these principles, which may have already elevated your story. Or it may indicate you are still too close to your work after all. That, too, is something you should know.

A Word of Caution from the Locker Room

Having just reviewed all twelve of the story elements and essences you graded earlier, you may be feeling that your revision is more work than you want to commit to. Certainly revising a story from a new narrative strategy is much more than a tweak—it's a rewrite. But maybe a rewrite is what you need to evolve your story into its highest form, because a rewrite is the best way to embrace all twelve realms (as listed herein) of possible revision at once. Just as you would do in a period of story planning for a first draft, study your story with a view toward making changes within your impending revision, and realize how many battlefronts that will entail. A page-one rewrite will be hard, but it can be blissful work, too, because you now know what you originally started with and how that story ended up, and hopefully you're much more aware of why it was rejected. Using that information, you can raise your story to a professional, publishable, salable standard, and perhaps beyond into the realm of excellence, by leveraging the tools and story physics at your disposal. A writer who experienced this best-case outcome might say, "Dang, I wish I'd known all this stuff when I wrote that earlier draft!"

May that be the outcome that awaits you.

If you don't know yet, keep hunting for the culprit in your narrative, and in your skills and belief systems about storytelling. Often a combination of these factors conspires to take your story down, and only with a holistic, empowered perspective that fuses story intentions and a heightened knowledge of craft can you survive and conquer those old tapes.

The single most dangerous thing you can do at this point is to fear the revision process itself. If you do, you must ask yourself this question: Is the story really worth it?

It very well might not be. You know so much more at this point than you did when you wrote your draft and perhaps when you started reading this book. Had you applied this level of criteria and standards to your original passion for your story, you might now feel differently about it. Maybe your story would have waited while you worked with it, strengthened it, and driven it toward something better using your broadened story sensibilities. I've written an entire chapter on this notion, which you'll encounter in the next section.

Either way, you win. Because if you are no longer in love with your story—not so much the story you wrote but the story you are going to write via the revision process—then your best call is to move on. Apply your enhanced awareness and skills to a new project that calls to you and won't leave you alone until you explore the possibilities.

At a recent writing conference, a keynote speaker, an agent out of New York, advised us to walk away from *all* of our story ideas. At least at first. When they tap your shoulder again, don't walk away, *run* away. Only when a story pursues you, tries to possess you, will it prove to be something worthy of your time and talents.

This makes total sense to me, and hopefully it will help explain your story issues if you jumped at an idea too soon. You have to love it back to make it work, to devote the time and courage and attention to detail—more detail than is humanly possible if you ascribe to thoughts that tumble helter skelter out of your head onto the page—before it becomes part of you in the way it needs to. You need to love it with not only your whole heart but your whole head. There is no such thing as "love at first sight" when it comes to story ideas. Allow the courtship to play out, vetting the idea on all fronts, including its staying power. Sometimes situations don't look as attractive the morning after a one-night stand.

Remember back in the beginning when I pounded on the very real possibility that your story, not your skill level, is the problem? Maybe now you can see this. Maybe you're already better than the story you set out to write.

Now you have the tools to make *that* call. Because the criteria for concept and premise become the benchmarks for a story idea that works … or doesn't.

Or maybe your story remains a challenging quest for you. It meets all of those criteria and is screaming to be written, ready to reward you in proportion to the focus and time you invest in it.

Like I said, either way, you win.

PART THREE
RESURRECTION

Seeking simplicity on the other side of complexity:
Once you know, you know.
The work isn't easier, but the path is clearer.

WELCOME TO THE SUCK

So here we are, grades in hand, definitions in place, criteria met, applications and stronger ideas ready to be implemented, concepts and premises re-examined and shored up. Maybe you feel that you now know what you didn't know before.

So let's talk.

Back when you wrote the draft you now realize needs fixing, you thought you were ready—to send it out into the world, to get it published. Revision will be difficult but perhaps more accessible now that you have tools, standards, and targeted benchmarks to work with.

But to make sure you're ready, let's look at what all this really means.

NOBODY LIKES TO TALK ABOUT REVISION

But that's why we're here, and already we're well down a contrarian path. But to fully embrace the revision process, we need to get your mind in the right place, myopically focusing on the formidable task of making your story *better* using a new and upgraded set of storytelling skills, tools, and principles.

I've given you several lists so far: six core competencies, six realms of story physics, three phases of story creation, two primary reasons your story isn't working, twelve elements to grade, and twelve opportunities for improvement.

I'm not done. And neither are you.

Here's another short list for you.

This one identifies criteria from the reader's side of the page and defines the things readers are looking for in a story, grouped into three categories. Readers don't care about plot points and realms of story physics as technical features; they care about the effect, the reading experience created by these tools. They are looking primarily for these three experiences, hoping for them from the moment they lay eyes on the first page of your book or screenplay.

The degree to which your story works is dependent on the degree to which your reader …

1. perceives **INTRIGUE** (becomes captivated) …
2. and **EMOTIONAL RESONANCE** (feels the weight of the stakes and is motivated to root for your hero with empathy) …
3. within a **VICARIOUS EXPERIENCE** (is transported into the story world).

Read those three items again, because the key to your revision may be hiding within them. While I'm betting that's the case, I'm also betting you've never heard those criteria grouped in this manner. You may notice that these are a subset of the six realms of story physics, but these are actually the *goals*. The other ingredients of story physics are the *means* of getting to them. By working with these goals to produce the desired reader outcome, you may avoid extensive revisions in the future.

Now you have a new and powerful context against which to evaluate all your choices as you consider what to fix in your story and how. Everything else, from character to structure to how you write sentences, is merely the pursuit of these three outcomes: *intrigue, emotional resonance, vicarious experience*. Both story selection and story execution rely on these target reader perceptions in order for them to become functional opportunities for the writer.

To paraphrase the iconic American novelist James Michener, he didn't believe he was a great writer but felt confident he was a really good *rewriter*. With this statement Michener was shining a light on how important revision is within the whole of the writing proposition. And as far as credibility is concerned, it doesn't get any better than James Michener.

He wasn't talking about proofreading, which is the correction of typos and punctuation and grammatical missteps. Rather, he was reflecting on *the revision of story* and the major tenets of craft that put that revised version onto the page. He was talking about moving things around, cutting sections, upgrading the core ideas, and adding depth and resonance where needed.

Revision requires two focuses in terms of process, both of which apply to the story level *and* the execution level of viability:

1. the identification and *repair* of that which is broken within a story, either at the story level or the narrative arc level
2. the *elevation* of that which has yet to reach its highest dramatic strength and character potential

In other words, we are looking for what's broken and what's just plain weak.

Here's an analogy: Two singers go to a vocal coach. One can't carry a tune but can really belt it out. The other has perfect pitch but no emotional depth or performance style. If you could combine them you'd have a star of Celine Dion proportions, but in reality both are faced with compromises. Both require correction if they aspire to sing professionally.

The first singer must fix what is broken. The second must improve to a professional level of artful performance.

For writers, both shortcomings are common. The repair and elevation required, once achieved, are equally valuable, to an extent that the story *depends* on them to work. The former gets you onto the concert stage; the latter can plaster your name across the Billboard 200. But a failure in either keeps you stuck in the corner pub singing karaoke.

Repair or elevation?

The first order of revision is to accurately assess which of those two opportunities for upgrade are on the table. Most revisions entail something from both realms. Are you revising story execution (one or more of the six core competencies), or are you beefing up something that is holding the story back (one or more of the six realms of story physics)? Knowing the difference creates an empowered context for your revision efforts.

As discussed in chapter one, the line blurs between fixing what is broken and jacking up what could simply be stronger. This challenges us to take care not to screw up something that is already working by tinkering with something that isn't.

When I wrote this chapter, the 2014 World Series had just ended. The MVP pitcher for the Giants, Madison Bumgarner, began his career with raw potential, but as soon as he arrived in camp as a young rookie, the coaches tried to change everything about his delivery. This was a big deal, because for pitchers the physics of delivery is everything. They sent him to the low minor leagues, where he got lit up like a Vegas casino sign. It didn't work, raw potential be damned. Every ballplayer, at every level of professional baseball, has some degree of raw potential. So, in the face of disappointing results, he decided to go back to who he was, to do his thing his way. The rest is history: He's become one of the premier pitchers in all of baseball.

Be sure to glean the right point from this analogy. He didn't mess with the underlying physics of what generates power in his pitches, or with what works for *any* pitcher. In fact, those physics were strengthened through this growth process. Those principles—finding the throwing slot, balance, reach, lower-body power—are untouchable. He simply found a way to make them work for *him* in a business that offers conventional wisdom from all angles. Just like you might be doing with your story, he tweaked his delivery to fall *more* solidly within the confines of his craft, in the way that best suited him, rather than trying to reinvent it according to the wishes of his well-meaning coaches.

Not all professionals do things the same way. There are story planners, outliners, drafters, organic writers, writers who listen to plants, whatever. But at the end of the writing day, when they succeed, they will have all observed the same fundamental principles of their craft.

A great story is like a house of cards.

Each level bears weight and demands artful balance, and when you swap out one card for another the whole thing teeters for a while, until you make it work. The principles of gravity and balance are the only forces available to make revising that house of cards successful.

REVISION IS AN INEVITABILITY

And for many, revision is as unpleasant as it is necessary. We prefer to think of it as *editing*, a polite and imprecise word that, without keener context, focuses more on grammar and punctuation. We actually should be calling it by other names: damage control, repair, resurrection. Make no mistake—the goal is simply to *fix* the thing, whether that means stitching open wounds or building muscle.

Revision and copyediting—the latter being *editing* in its most common context—require vastly different skill sets. Confuse the two during your story-fixing efforts and you will be, in the words of my son, toast. Copyediting should usually be farmed out to specialists; most writers stink up the copyediting phase when they try to save a buck and do it themselves. But *story-level* revision remains squarely in your lap as the author, even with seemingly precise input to work from. The issues it addresses are of your creation, and now you get to correct and/or improve them.

One of the best things you can do is pay a professional to tell you, without flinching, how your story could be better. If you can't sense it yourself—which is a very tall order for the newer writer—I highly recommend consulting a professional. Your critique group or your fellow unpublished writing buddies may not have the evolved story sensibilities required to accurately peg what needs improvement, and they may provide *opinions* that aren't as easily perceived or understood as a professional diagnosis. For example, if they say, "It just never got off the ground for me. You never captured my imagination," you have no real clue if the problem was that the story itself was flat, or that you bungled the execution relative to pacing via structure. A pro, however, would nail down that issue for you.

To revise the story successfully, you'll need to *know.*

Within the public context of the writing conversation—conferences, workshops, craft books, critique groups, writers' groups, or even the caffeine gang at Starbucks—we regard the revision process as a means of closure, the simple finishing of a job. We can compare it to cleaning up paint or (perhaps more apropos) mopping up blood after surgery. The cleanup process itself is part of, identical to, or simply an extension of the process by which the original version was created in the first place.

Tell that to the nurse scrubbing the operating room floor after the doctor has departed to make his tee time.

And yet it isn't the same. Your *process*—the way you think and the beliefs you hold—contributed to the draft that now requires fixing, so doing the same thing to repair and upgrade it can be an exercise in frustration leading to another level of failure. Revision at the story level has to summon *more* craft—or even a unique flavor of craft—that stems from a keener story awareness than the process that created the original version now lying on the operating table.

Why is this true?

Because at the point of revision we know *more* about the story, which is the patient in this diagnosis and curing process. It is now a whole-cloth, front-to-back version of itself, which allows both strengths and weaknesses to shine in a way they couldn't while dwelling in the clutter and confusion of original construction. As you write, you are immersed in a forest of options. Only when you move away from that forest can you see its trees, including the ones that are about to tumble over.

Here's a fact, something writers don't want to embrace until their story takes a critical hit: You can't successfully execute a story arc, you can't foreshadow and build tension and creative deception and conflict, *until* you know as much about the story as there is to know. And the most important aspect of that is knowing how the story will end.

You know that now. You may not have known it as you wrote, because you may not have been writing in context to an ending you were intimately familiar with or confident about. Which may very well have been the problem.

That ending is now your new beginning.

Any draft written without the context of a defined, targeted ending will be less than adequate. This happens all the time with professional writers who develop their stories using drafting (rather than planning), but rest assured, when they finish a draft that works, it will have a clear vision for the ending in place from page 1. The draft that didn't have an ending in mind was written, in part, for that express purpose: to find the best possible way and means to resolve the story.

Maybe intuitive story arc geniuses like Stephen King and Nora Roberts can do it—and you could, too, after you've written a garage full of completed novels—but the truth is, this isn't normal or easy. Nor is it likely. It isn't the case for you or me. And because we don't really know how many hands touch those best-selling, A-list stories, or how many drafts it took to get there, it may not be normal or easy for them either.

A great many story issues arise from drafts in which the ending wasn't clear until the writer got to it. That's why the retrospective ten thousand-foot view, the one that shows the weak spots from a draft already in place, is supremely illuminating.

And yet, there are writers who begin a draft not knowing how the story will end. That is their process and their prerogative. No one knows how many of those drafts lead to an ending that works, with a path that requires little tinkering. That insight never makes it into the interviews with writers who work this way, which means that we learn little from those writers about the process itself.

The odds could be low for you, too. This could explain what's not working in your story. Did you discover your ending mid-draft? Does your story initially push forward without the context of a specific ending seeping between the lines, allowing for foreshadowing, the building of the optimal story beats and nuances that support that eventual ending? When you do finally know how it ends, does the exposition suddenly come alive with that context, at the point in the story where you finally figured it out? And, if that's the case, is the narrative less alive up until that epiphany?

If so, you probably need another draft.

And if you didn't write that new draft, if you submitted the draft in which the ending came to you somewhere in the middle, then that explains why it isn't working as a whole front-to-back story. It was your process as much as your manuscript.

This can be the easiest revision of all.

With a head full of fresh new craft, just start over, line by line, using your complete contextual awareness of the ending as context for evaluating what you see. Ask what could be better within that higher context. You can now imbue your story with foreshadowing, irony, and deeper stakes, all of which were impossible within a draft that didn't know where it was headed.

It can be as simple as this. Compare an operation, a surgery, performed by someone who has not gone to medical school with a procedure done by someone who has. Or, even better, a surgery performed by a recent graduate compared to the same surgery undertaken by someone with thirty years of experience.

Knowledge and an evolved story sensibility are precisely what it takes to write stories that work over the course of a career. Wrestling with both elements is what it takes to make a story work at the early stages of a career.

Be clear: This isn't an indictment of how you got there. Using a draft to find your story—including how it ends—is viable and very common. Just don't label that draft *final* in any way, shape, or form, because the legitimately *final* draft needs to have the ending in mind from square one.

Or you could just plan it out ahead of time.

It's hard to argue with writers who claim they can't plan a story until they are in the midst of writing it. That's their claim—who are we to argue? But rare is the writer who can successfully *revise* a story with the same level of well-intended blindness by simply going through the pages without a clear mission in mind.

Many writers have discovered that you don't have to actually write a draft to ascertain the terrain of your story, ending included. And here, on the cusp of revision, you should take a page from their handbook and do the same. Plan your revision. Revise in context to what you *know* is wrong or weak in your story. Target those weaknesses with specificity and with the context of the principles that will help you diagnose the problem and solve it. A process of in-depth story planning works just as well for many writers at the story origin stage, and even when the writer generated the revisable draft organically. Story planning, applied as a process of revision, is often the ticket out of that fog.

Story planning is nothing other than coming up with and vetting options for story beats in a linear fashion across the arc of the story. It's literally making up and playing out the story in your head, then taking notes on how it goes down. This is *exactly* what pantsers (organic writers) do when they use drafting as the chosen process of searching for and landing upon the story, except the vetting is rarely included. Instead they trust their story instincts in that moment of decision and plow forward from there, writing directly from their head. The two processes are more alike than advocates of either are sometimes willing to admit.

If you're a pantser and believe story planning is impossible—because it's impossible *for you*—then you've just come face to face with a limiting belief, one that will evolve, by the way, as you increase your knowledge about how stories work. If this is you, staring down the barrel of an impending revision, perhaps another look at that belief will serve you well.

Almost every proud pantser with a track record will admit, under oath perhaps, that they do a good amount of story planning as they go. Only for them it happens in their mind rather than in an outline, which means it is only a technicality that they *don't outline*, because in truth they did. In your head or on a flowchart, or on a wall full of yellow sticky notes, story planning by any other name is useful to all writers.

Trust me, Stephen King and Nora Roberts and Diana Gabaldon and other famous pantsers really *do* know where their stories are going when they finally set out to write the draft that ends up being published. Those prior "search" drafts are the equivalent of notes. Those notes have now become the plan itself.

10

IS YOUR STORY WORTH SAVING?

Did he really just ask that?

This chapter is for those of you who, even after exploring all the principles and criteria and analogies, still nurse a sneaking suspicion that your story may be just fine as is.

Indeed it might be. Then again, change is always hard, and sometimes we are immune to that realization because *we* are the ones who need to change. After nine bulging chapters on craft, you may be equipped to view your original story idea, and the concept and premise that evolved from it, with a more evolved story sensibility. Things might look different to you now.

REJECTION ... LET US COUNT THE WAYS

Agents and editors have infinite ways and means to justify and defend as they reject the stories submitted to them. Most are polite, even more are concise, and a few are rendered with an iciness that bumps up against outright cruelty. But very few will tell you, as part of the rejection litany, that your story may, indeed, not be worth saving at all.

And yet, that may very well be the case.

If it is, the scope of your rejection takes on a new dimension. For it to work, you may need to revise your story at its most fundamental levels, until the thing actually becomes a different story altogether. When feedback leads to changing the very core of the idea itself, and touches virtually all levels, core competencies, and means of evoking a reader response, something else is actually afoot, an unspoken inevitability that needs to be acknowledged.

In that case, you may simply need to start over with a different, better story idea.

You won't hear this advice at a writing conference.

The prevailing context at writing retreats and conferences, sung to the melody of "Kumbaya," is that any story can be spun into gold with enough time, effort, and craft. What's missing is the fine print that says a deeper level of understanding will actually turn the current story into *another* story altogether. How so? Because more powerful criteria will then be applied, most likely at the source and level of dramatic tension, which is the sweet spot of a story's inherent potential.

If your computer is too underpowered to run new software, and you replace the key components that deliver speed, graphics, and memory to the extent that none of the original parts remain, is the end product still the same computer? To people who understand that world, it's not, even if the screen and the keyboard and the logo on the monitor look the same as before.

When you first faced the blank page, you chose your story for reasons that made sense to you at the time. Think, for instance, of a young child who, while riding in the car on the road to a family vacation, announced that she wanted to be a fire engine when she grew up. She just *didn't know* that this wasn't such a great plan. And so you tell the child that, while perhaps a sweet sentiment, becoming a fire engine won't work. Not ever. The next day, you ask the child what she wants to be when she grows up, expecting a revised answer that will work. But how can that happen if the child isn't basing the revision of her answer on a richer life experience seasoned with mentoring and patience? Without mentoring within the learning moment? No, on the next day, instead of a fire engine, the child will proudly announce she wants to be a soccer ball, because soccer is fun.

That analogy is more apt than you might think. I know this after years of reviewing the story intentions of perfectly sane and mature adults, each of whom thought they had landed on a winner.

Too often we choose too quickly.

"Of course my story is worth saving."

It's mine. Nobody can, or should, tell me it's not worth the time to try to save it. This is what we tell ourselves. Indeed, it is worth saving, if the question of its worth is posed within a noble *this-is-art* context.

Think of it this way: A guy in your neighborhood might choose to paint his house in a red plaid pattern and tell everyone to just deal with it. You can't do anything about this; he's Scottish, he thinks it looks great, and it's his house. Nobody says anything, and everyone just drives by a plaid house every day on the way home from work. But if that guy aspires to be a professional designer, then his tastes and belief system relative to what works and what doesn't *in that neighborhood* become the problem, because despite what he thinks, it just isn't working.

Millions of rejected writers belong to the red-plaid club. Read the case studies in Part Four of this book, and you'll see this truth manifest before your eyes. You'll also gain an explanation for why it doesn't work.

You get to decide. The trick is to empower yourself by making better choices. Use the criteria and benchmarks for what constitutes a compelling and effective story in today's market. Take a look at the feasibility and scope of a target readership that might share your enthusiasm, and then plant your story flag. Make an enlightened decision about the viability of your story, instead of an emotional one. Don't cling to something you, as an author, have evolved beyond.

Story sensibility is everything. And it first shows up when the writer declares what the story will be.

THE FIRST DECISION POINT OF REVISION

A story needs to be worth saving, and we need to understand the criteria for making that decision. If finding a readership isn't the goal, if the writer needs to write this story for personal, cathartic reasons, then it absolutely is worth saving. There is more than one reason to write a novel. But if getting published and building a writing career is the goal, then a higher standard applies.

A story is built from a compelling concept, even when that concept wasn't the starting point. Not all concepts are created equal. Great concepts meet certain criteria, separating them from lesser concepts.

For some, revision is the means of finding that concept or raising it (by evolving it) to meet the criteria that were unmet in the earlier draft.

Now that you are on the other side of wondering, now that you know, let's return to square one and review what works and what doesn't. See if it all looks a little different to you.

VETTING THE FEEDBACK THAT BROUGHT YOU HERE

If the issue of story worthiness confronts you, it's because somebody has suggested that the story is weak at some point, perhaps at its very core, irrespective of execution and the crystalline brilliance of your sentences (though your sentences and execution may have been the target of criticism, too.) It's all just opinion, of course, so you confront a crossroads at the moment an opinion arrives. Who is telling you this, and why might you want to pay attention? A story about a serial killer might not appeal to your very religious sibling, who says, "Your story just doesn't work for me, but your writing is really terrific!" Pay attention at this point, because you are alone in deciding how to proceed. And everything depends on your decision.

A story about trying to make it to Walmart before closing time (that one crossed my desk a while ago, intended as a metaphor for living a chaotic, modern life) will likely never become the iconic literature of self-actualization you first imagined it would be.

Really, though, sometimes such an assessment in the harshest degree—even when it's fair and accurate—is more an issue of *semantics* than it is a pronouncement of death. Even when the feedback is intended to kill your story.

Anything can be revised.
Revision isn't as simple as showing up. You have to do more than show up. You have to stand out when you get there.

It's not uncommon for a writer to realize that absolutely everything in the proposed story must be rethought and rebooted. But at a certain point, a hammer melted down and recast to look like a screwdriver has *become* a screwdriver. So don't let the semantics of *revision* versus *replacement* fool you—if the story is weak at its core, you probably need another story.

When you realize this, you aren't defying the agent or publisher or story coach who thought your story wasn't worth saving. Actually, when you decide the story must change to the extent that it's suddenly another story altogether, you're in agreement. This is common, and it's good. The natural marketplace is at work, applying the reader-driven forces of story to the draft. Your story didn't line up with those forces before. Now, post revision, it does.

Like people with a pulse, stories require certain minimum elements, essences, and chemistry to work. Within the realm of storytelling, deciding whether your piece has met those minimums is a matter of opinion—someone's opinion, and yours included. The idea of revision, the goal of it, is to arm *yourself* with the ability to refine that opinion into a more enlightening and empowering one than the belief you held when you wrote the criticized draft.

Even doctors in the ER have to make that call on dying patients. It's the point at which they look up at the clock, "call it," and then put away the paddles.

It doesn't matter what label you assign to the reboot process—first aid, polish, or resurrection from the dead. What matters is understanding *when* and *why* this discussion applies to you and what you need to *do* about it.

Sometimes the news that your story isn't good enough is the best news of all. Before, you probably thought it *was* good enough. The dispenser of that verdict has just, in some combination, given you new hope and a new future, and has saved you several months of pain and additional work. This pivotal moment of decision, and what you do about it, is a call that makes or breaks your writing dream.

THE BEARER OF BAD NEWS

As a story coach I stare down the throat of stories that need help every day. It's the nature of the story-coaching beast; if someone's writing didn't require coaching, it wouldn't be on my screen. Sometimes story coaching is like trying to turn a ninety-eight-pound weakling into the proud parent's vision of a first-round draft choice after only a few pushups and protein bars.

And yet, the only way to transform such a project is to whip up a Captain America level of resurrection. You'll recall that Captain America was once a ninety-eight-pound weakling named Steve Rogers who was given a super-soldier serum and transformed into a warrior with a new body, a new persona, and a new mission. Rogers wasn't "saved"; he was essentially *replaced*.

Should you save your story? Try to breathe life into it by medicating the symptoms instead of the cause?

Or should you reinvent it? That's the real question, and your make-or-break opportunity.

Sometimes it's a thumbs down.

More often than I care to say (and you really don't want to know), the degree of help required to make a story viable falls within the same realm as what the aforementioned Walmart novel would have needed. This was a story so lacking in weight (while at the same time burdened with the misguided thematic hubris of its creator) that it was like a newborn brought into the world without bones, muscle, blood, or even a brain.

Bones, muscle, blood, and a functioning brain are the minimum criteria of human life. Storytelling has a similar set of minimum criteria: a compelling premise, someone to root for, dramatic tension stemming from stakes, a vicarious experience, a sense of emotional engagement. Often they are too weak or missing altogether.

Skip one and you're dead in the water. Maybe that's what happened to your story. Maybe that list can swing open the curtains of your awareness about what went wrong and what you need to focus on in a revision cycle.

You've heard of beer goggles? It means that someone who looked attractive after a few beers at midnight doesn't look so lovely in the clear light of morning. Same thing with our stories: We need to view them in the clear light of our own heightened awareness about storytelling.

The problem is this: The writer has what he believes to be a cool notion for a story, but it's challenging, complicated, "out there." The writer isn't aware of that little checklist of bare minimum requirements. So he makes some leaps, asks the reader to suspend logic and disbelief, and inserts more stretches and concoctions just to connect dots that don't logically lead to each other. Before long, the writer has a story in which the CIA is coming to a shy fourteen-year-old math whiz with an alcoholic parent to save the world because, gosh darn it, there just aren't enough smart and capable trained adults sitting in windowless rooms in a CIA facility who can actually do that work and save the world themselves. Yeah, a kid with a laptop and a winning record in *Call of Duty* is clearly what we need.

If your wimpy teenage hero has to hack into National Security Agency servers to get the information required to save the world—because, of course, all fourteen-year-olds have that level of technical skill—then odds are your story is dead on arrival. It's been stretched and bent and contrived to death. It's absurd. You can't make it anything other than absurd. It's a house built on sand in a windstorm.

Clinging to a story like this one is like lying. You tell one gigantic lie, and then you need to heap lie after lie on top of the original whopper to hold the whole teetering tower together. But, oh, that first lie … it was so beautiful. If only it were true. Maybe people will overlook the absurdity of it all and accept it as true. And so you bend all logic and reason to make it assumptively logical in your story world.

How you think, as much as what you think, has just tanked your story.

But here's the deal: You can't turn a poor story idea into an excellent story, and you can't transform your nonheroic, sad-sack protagonist with a pathetic backstory into someone readers will gladly root for, without replacing that idea and that backstory with a stronger concept that inspires less head-scratching.

Bend all you want, but bending and stretching the prevailing logic kills your story as much as a premise that makes people roll their eyes. And that's not on the story—it's on you. Logic bending is the Great Abyss of pantsing, because in the moment you can't see the story-consuming forest for the illogical trees you've planted.

The trouble with the business of writing publishable fiction is that we're often reaching for a moving, imprecise, often invisible bar. This is why some good writers who try don't actually succeed. And it's why some writers—the professional storytellers who have earned the name tag, not because of track record but because of their level of craft—eventually do.

RETURNING TO YOUR DRAMATIC QUESTION

The story's dramatic question works when it is compelling without the need to bend it into something else entirely, something that makes absolutely no sense (like a normal fourteen-year-old kid hacking into CIA servers). The trick is to imbue your story with the kind of DNA that gives it a shot. It needs to make sense, even if your entire story world doesn't. Too many writers have deluded themselves into believing they've succeeded, when in fact their ship is taking on water and won't make it out of the harbor into the open ocean. When a dramatic question is primarily thematic rather than dramatic, the reader is left wondering what to root for within the narrative itself.

When you write a story, you own the conceit that you know what readers will find compelling. Think about that for a moment ... and then look in a mirror and ask yourself if you really do know what readers want.

Impossibility vs. Absurdity

It is a fatal mistake to attempt to breathe life into a story by bending and stretching the reader's capacity to believe. Readers want to believe, but in your passion for the story you can stretch that belief too far. You ask them to accept the absurd or to stick around while you show them a bunch of nonessential backstory and character building and sideshows before getting back to the pursuit of an answer to that all-important dramatic question.

It's fine to ask them to accept the impossible—bookstores and movie theaters are full of those stories, and they work because the leap you suggest shines a light on something very real. As a career-saving rule, writers need to draw a line between the impossible and the absurd, and stick to the artistically viable and transparent side of that line.

It boils down to a simple question: Is your core story landscape and the premise that you set upon it cool and provocative, even if it is actually impossible? Let me answer that with another question: Did Star Trek work? Were the concept and premise of the television show and blockbuster films impossible in the real world?

Impossibility may be part of the fun. Absurdity, however, is part of the reason something gets tossed.

The absurd is often defended as an analogy or a metaphor for reality. The novels of Tom Robbins come to mind—they shine a light on the truly absurd happenings in real life that surround us all. This is where the crowd thins out, because these kinds of stories are among the most difficult to pull off in all of literature. If you are writing in the absurdity niche, which is a second cousin of parody and fraught with risk, and if you've been rejected, then you need to accept the judgment that the story and its execution just aren't good enough. "Good enough" in this arena is a very high bar. You need to do better.

Can any story work?

This story arrived on my desk recently: What if mankind is descended from a race of alien insects, and we all have within us a dormant bit of DNA that suddenly springs to life in response to our polluted water supply?

Wow. Where the hell did that idea come from? And how do you rationalize it as a sign of our times? Try as I might, I couldn't find a reasonable metaphoric connection to anything in reality. The premise catered to a room full of intoxicated fanboys looking for escapist fare.

If you can't defend absurdity other than to say, "But it's so cool!" you are on tricky ground. Absurdity only works when you convince the reader to simply roll with it and/or to find a higher meaning in it. And that is something you cannot take for granted. If you've been rejected with a story like this, perhaps that higher meaning escaped your reader.

Regardless of what you believe, if your concept is perceived as absurd by agents or editors, it is already DOA, no matter how well you've written it. When in doubt, you need to hear it from the perspective of another professional, someone who knows the difference between a player who belongs on the field and one who needs to stay in the bleachers.

The Fix

The only thing you can do to prevent readers from dismissing your story as absurd is to gain a heightened awareness of what makes a story *work*. In other words, you need a story sensibility that arises from, and is built upon, the inherent potential for story physics and then rendered with solid mechanics. It depends on the nature of the concept and the way that concept fuels and empowers a premise. If the concept and premise have enough energy and potential and freshness in their DNA, they just might give the story a chance at a bright future.

To wit: Dramatic tension arises from a compelling dramatic question, connecting to a hero who must do something in pursuit of a worthy goal, with something blocking the straight line toward the goal, and with something at stake. That's it, in the proverbial nutshell. You should memorize it, make it a mantra, because this is the whole ballgame in one sentence.

If any of those composite parts is missing or weak in your story, hopefully you are feeling a little buzz deep in your stomach. That's the truth trying to escape and slap you upside the head with a new awareness that will save your story and your writing dream.

Is writing still a dream if you accept that you can't write your story any damn way you please? Or, after all is said and done, in this gloomy world of craft and criteria and staggering odds, is writing actually work?

As they say in the lottery business, adjust your dreams accordingly.

In the real world even 100 million dollars won't buy you a city of gold populated by fairies and dragons, because those things defy the physics of our reality. Stories have principles of physics as well, and they are inviolate. Absurdity without drama—absurdity that exists solely because the author doesn't recognize the absurdity or just thinks it's really cool—is not the stuff of dreams. It is the stuff of illusion and self-deception.

When the goal is to render those narrative physics on the page, it happens only from a solid foundation of storytelling craft that seizes the inherent dramatic potential of the concept/premise promise and molds it into narrative gold.

The trick resides in recognizing what the winning concept/premise DNA consists of (which I just told you), then summoning the requisite craft to bring it to fruition over the arc of a story that is artfully assembled and rendered.

You can be dead right.

Emphasis on *dead*.

You can get all six core competencies right, and the story can still sink like a stone tied to the foot of a protagonist who never stood a chance. You can put makeup and clothes on a store mannequin to make it look like a person, to make it beautiful and mesmerizing, but you still can't make it walk across a room.

That's what happens when you check off the criteria boxes as applied to a lukewarm concept and premise. Our job as writers is to pick the right story, the best story. The one that stands a chance in hell in a business in which there really doesn't seem to be a chance at all, if the statistics are to be believed.

Life is too short to waste time breathing life into something that is truly, absolutely dead. Sometimes it's better to give birth to something new instead.

11

SPINNING HOPE FROM REJECTION

WELCOME TO THE BERMUDA TRIANGLE OF STORYTELLING

Your story is a vessel. It must float on a sea of possibility. If the weight of absurdity, familiarity, or underachievement is too heavy, the boat will sink. The relationship between an idea, a concept, and a premise defines the Bermuda Triangle of storytelling, where well-intentioned writers too often set sail without the right navigation, sensibility, or awareness to avoid being swallowed alive.

Surviving these deadly waters requires more than knowing how to swim (i.e., how to write nice sentences), or having an interesting idea alone. It's knowing how to navigate the waters of a story with a vessel that is strong and seaworthy.

After reading the chapters thus far, this is, of course, old news. But what remains floating is perhaps our willingness to embrace it all, to allow the principles to flow in as our limited beliefs are dumped overboard. That, like storytelling itself, is sometimes a hard thing to accomplish.

There's a reason why revision is so freaking hard.

But if you think about it, it shouldn't be. With all these principles and tools, it should at least be *manageable*. The damage is sitting in the rejected draft, staring back at you, mocking you, or it's ringing in your ears from an outside source. The upside should position revision as more of a gift than a burden, but that's sometimes hard to see, because you are either in denial, or you know it was you who did it that way in the first place, working with the best intentions and without the slightest clue you were mismanaging the moment. So now, armed only with a new awareness, perhaps a need you don't even understand, you're supposed to suddenly bring something different to the process of fixing it?

This is craziness in its purest form.

If you're a professional writer seeking representation from an agent, or to land a contract from a publisher, or even just to earn a little buzz in the crowded wilderness of self-published fiction, then one thing is beyond argument: Rejection hurts. It sucks on so many levels, even though the public writing conversation has assured you this was coming, because it always does. It still hurts.

And yet, despite the pain, and unlike so many other avocations that we embrace because they are fun and personally (versus professionally) rewarding, rejection matters. Hey, we believe we're pretty good at the stuff we do personally: dancing, karaoke, golf, painting, poker, knitting, ping pong, bodybuilding, cooking. You can play crappy golf or tennis or bridge every weekend for the rest of your life, and it doesn't change your experience or alter your future. You're still having a good time. But this isn't the case with writing. We thrive on hope, on the belief that our efforts are actually leading us toward something.

Pain exists not because it is an issue of winning or losing but rather because it is a measure of personal identity and ambition. Rejection threatens our dream. But that perception is exactly backwards. Rejection reminds us how *hard* this is, dashing hope in the process, and yet perhaps fueling us with an ambition that seeks to find an upside.

While you likely wouldn't think to declare yourself a professional in your weekend recreational pursuits, as a writer, otherwise worldly and wise, you might consider yourself a professional even now. You go to writing conferences, start writing books, seek representation, and suddenly, because you absolutely *do* intend to sell your work, you bestow upon yourself the mantle of the *professional*. Which means— and here is a rarely spoken truth—you are competing with everyone else at the writing conference, if for nothing else than mindshare and respect from agents and editors. The respect and props you seek from them are defined by how your story compares to everyone else's.

But you opted in as a professional, not a weekend warrior. Which means you don't get to take it personally. For the enlightened professional, the call for revision becomes an opportunity rather than a reminder of your limitations.

And yet, it seems so ... daunting.

What you hear at the writing conference, particularly when it comes to the revision process, may not take you where you want to go. Not because the advice you pick up is wrong, per se, but because it can be imprecise. It comes at you in pieces, little chunks of conventional wisdom floating alone and unconnected—as from a workshop on how to write better dialogue, for example—on a sea of assumed, yet less-than-clear, relevance to a bigger picture.

So you're saying better dialogue will make my novel better? The answer is: Sure it will. Always. But then there's this slightly different question: *So you're saying that writing better dialogue will get me published?*

This is why many writers drink.

And why writing teachers exist at the very edge of madness.

The bigger picture will save you.

When your story requires revision, chances are something you've done doesn't fully align with the principles that show us how a story works, and it can be found at the story level rather than the craft level.

The sow's ear, chicken-droppings level.

Listen closely ... that sound in your head may be your inner author trying to tell you something. And chances are you really need to hear it.

The more you know about the craft of storytelling, the louder that voice becomes. The more you know about storytelling—both at the story level and the craft level—the clearer the message itself will be.

Our profession is full of writers who hear the call. They acknowledge doubt in the form of that inner voice telling them something is off the mark, but they don't really know how to respond. Usually they respond by submitting their work somewhere else to see what happens, hoping to confirm their suspicion that the first agent or editor was having a bad day.

And then it comes back to them with the same outcome. And the voice telling those writers to revise becomes louder and more impatient.

The enlightened writer listens.

You've been introduced to the tools, criteria, and benchmarks of a strong story that can be applied to the revision process, as well as to a first draft. Maybe you haven't yet internalized them. Maybe you zoned out when they were being presented at the writing conference. Maybe you opted for the session on how to land an agent instead. Maybe you prefer the indulgent musings of keynote speakers who wax eloquent about the mystery of it all, the muse that channels through them, the characters that speak to them, the immersion in their process with the trust that somehow, some way, someday, their story will finally make sense.

Here's a newsflash for those writers who like to tell their friends that there is something mystical in what we do: There are no actual muses (there are *inspirations*, which are different animals), and your characters don't talk to you. When stories are broken—they are very much like friends and relatives and politicians in this regard—they're not going to confess their sins and give you a strategy for healing. No, the voices you ascribe to muses and talking characters are just *you*, speaking to yourself from a place of story sensibility, which is the sum and nuance of all you've read and studied and concluded on your writing journey. You'll finally hear it—it'll sound a lot like an improved sense of story when you do—because it makes sense to you. Because you've had your fill of pain and frustration, and you're finally opening up to higher thinking.

SEEKING THE SWEET SPOT

I offer this next point from my experience presenting writing workshops for the last twenty-five years. Writers arrive in the room with certain belief systems about writing that define what is and isn't true in their minds. This causes them to be resistant to anything that challenges those beliefs and leads to a rather strong sense of confidence that what they've written, or intend to write, is rock solid and infused with genius. When something challenges that assumption—like someone saying that your characters don't talk to you, or that there may be a better path for your story—they shut down to some extent. They are processing the contradictions, the perception of falsehood hanging in the air, and thus don't completely perceive the meaning and inherent opportunity in what's being presented.

Some readers of this book will, at this point, not clearly comprehend a critical nuance: that the process of story fixing isn't just for rejected books, it's for any story that seeks to become a better story. And complicating this is the cold, hard truth that some rejected books aren't necessarily broken at all; they simply may not have landed in the sweet spot, at the right time, of their publishing journey. In this sense, revision is merely a form of starting over, building your best story from the inside out, from the ground up, from the truth of the principles that will never steer you wrong.

TO REVISE, OR NOT TO REVISE

Then again, every rejection slip does not necessarily signal the need for a major revision. Your story may be perfectly fine as is. The rejection may come from a source you do not understand and therefore do not value. More often, though, harsh criticism and rejection may actually be the wake-up call the writer needs. And thus, it's on the shoulders of the writer to know the difference—timing rather than a lack of sufficient craft—and to use feedback in all its forms to accurately assess the story's strengths and weaknesses and apply that feedback to move forward accordingly. The tools and processes apply to any origin of the need for story repair, however it is conveyed—be it a rejection or simply a depressing hunch that won't leave you alone.

Worthy stories, some of which go on to success, certainly do get rejected all the time, both by agents and publishers. They are the stuff of urban legend. Do a quick Google search and you'll find them everywhere. I'll mention again the quote from esteemed author William Goldman: "Nobody knows anything."

It's too true. But it's also a risky way to place your bet. Because you could rationalize the rejection of your story as simply a case of timing or another agent who doesn't get it rather than a legitimate red flag that should get your attention. We can be sure that Kathryn Stockett didn't revise her manuscript forty-six times, one for each instance of rejection. But because she hasn't talked about it, we can't say for sure how those rejections colored her subsequent sequence of drafts, if at all.

Right here is where a paradox kicks in: If you don't possess the knowledge to nail it the first time out, and are now stuck with the need to revise, how can you leverage feedback and rejection in the writing of a subsequent draft to solve those problems? You're the same writer who wrote that flawed story. How can you suddenly, without elevating your skill set, attempt to hoist good toward greatness? That's like asking a toddler who has just fallen off his bicycle to simply get back up and try it again, without showing him what went wrong. A lot of fathers have tried just that method over the years—"It builds character," they say—and it's always a recipe for further frustration and tears, as well as a few Band-Aids.

You can't expect to take your story higher with the same skill set as before, at least to the extent that you don't understand the feedback itself. But you're here, you're learning the unique tools and principles that drive successful revision, and that just might change everything about your next swing at the story.

As professional writers we are beyond the need to use our work as a means of personal character building. We require *knowledge* applied toward the growth of something much more amorphous and elusive: a heightened storytelling sense.

You can no longer be a suffering artist first and foremost, and a professional writer, too.

A starving professional writer, perhaps, but suffering is optional in the professional realm, because there are tools and principles to rely on. Suffering artists can, and do, create their own boundaries and standards for their craft. They can blame those chatty muses they're always listening to, and in essence they may choose to believe they can do this thing called writing any way they choose. Because it is art. Market expectations and principles be damned. But even the most ardent followers of organic craft align with the principles that make a story work, so process really isn't the question at all, at any level. Criteria, benchmarks, and principles are what matter, combined with passion, vision, and the perseverance that is surely part of the job description.

Having a truly killer story idea doesn't hurt either.

In the long and dark list of reasons why a story doesn't work, why it gets rejected and requires extensive repair, the writer's need to suffer is a common seed of dysfunction. It leads to procrastination, the claim of unfairness, and an ignorance of the options. Writers who don't summon the context of the principles of craft as part of their story sensibility, who go about it in the belief they can invent the structures and tropes and forces that make stories work, tend to populate the roster of the rejected, and sadly, colonize the roster of the self-published, casting a shadow over the multitude of very fine self-published books right next to them.

Even when this happens to a small degree, success becomes elusive.

Your art, in this case, wrapped in the limiting paradox of your process, often becomes your excuse for not finding an agent, or not selling when you do. "They just don't get me" is the graveside plea of the unpublished, unprofessional writer. While, in the meantime, the professional writer stays in the trenches to learn what went wrong and how to fix it.

CHOOSING TO SUCCEED

Ever notice how, at writing conferences that present lots of choices for sessions and presenters, there is rarely a session on *how to know if your story idea is good enough*? I've been to hundreds of these things, and I've never seen this one. Instead they ask you to bring your story with you—the good, the bad, and the ugly—and listen to feedback relative to its execution rather than its core conceptual substance.

It's all craft, craft, craft. And on one level, that's how it should be.

But on another level, conceptual appeal is at least half of the whole ballgame. It's the half that can wreck you before you even throw the first pitch. We've spent several chapters pounding that home, and here it resurfaces as context for the bigger picture of story fixing.

Let me be clear: I'm a huge proponent of craft. I hope that much is obvious by now. Much of my website and both of my prior writing books offer a focus on all of the various facets of the storytelling craft. But we're missing the boat if that's where the knowledge begins and ends, because craft is only half of the available rationale for rejecting a story.

THE TRUTH HURTS

When we don't dare to speak about the very real possibility that a story idea, *your idea*, may be dull as dirt, that it might be dead on arrival, we are stepping over the body to examine the crime scene. This is the epitome of what publishers mean when they say, *It's too familiar … it didn't bowl me over … it's lacking X, Y, and Z.* They're criticizing your story, not your writing.

They're saying the *story* isn't strong enough. And when *that's* the case—because high craft cannot save a weak story—your execution skills are rendered moot. Good writing is always a good thing, but it's rarely *the* thing that will get you published.

It's like being told your kid is too ugly to be a model, even though she knows how to walk a runway. Or that she's too slow and uncoordinated to be an athlete, even though she knows the rules of the game.

Story is a qualitative assessment. You can't measure it. It is always an opinion, beginning with yours at the moment of its creation. And so the best you can do is try to contextualize the nature and scope of the ways in which stories appeal to, or don't appeal to, target readerships.

As a professional, it's no longer about *you*. It's about your readers. Grasping that flip in context can save your writing dream. It is that suffering, unpublished, unread writer who continues to cry out that writing is art, her art, and she writes what pleases her. Meanwhile, the successful writer finds his pleasure in writing stories that touch other lives and gain a spreading readership.

But that dirty little secret remains. At the edge of frustration, possibly explaining why your novel was rejected, is this: Your story idea may not be good enough.

But nobody will tell you that.

It's too … unspeakable. And you don't want to hear it. How dare they? It's opinion, nothing more. It's nobody's business to tell you what your story should be about. That's your choice, and it's personal. There are no rules; you can and should write about any damn thing you want. This is art, for goodness sake.

Thus goes the lament of the rejected writer still clinging to his *art*.

I know why, too. Because I've been the guy who actually says it, face to suddenly pale face. I've sat across from writers in one-on-one situations at workshops after reading their synopsis in some form and told them in as clear and kind a manner as possible that their story is weak, that it won't fly.

I hate that moment. The look I get is more confusion than pain, because nobody has told them anything like this before. As if nobody *should* tell them. As if it just cannot be true. And yet, my job as a story coach is to identify and work on what will hold a story back, and often it's right there in the pitch, logline, or statement of premise.

The story just isn't *there*.

What happens next is all over the board. Usually they listen, or pretend to listen, then search for a contrary opinion, or at least for someone who can tell them how to make their sack-of-potatoes story into a bag of gold.

I could tell them that, too, and often do. It can be done. Using the criteria for a good story, one needs to let go of the old story and allow it to evolve into something stronger. Instead they usually try to explain why their pitch or synopsis doesn't sound good and assure me that if I read the entire manuscript I would see that it works.

Some just tune me out and move on. *Time wasted*, they think. *He just didn't get it.* That could be true. It's just opinion, after all. But after years of doing this, I have a pretty good nose for a story that stinks.

WHAT STORY *IS*, AND WHAT IT ISN'T

Writers who don't know what a story is tend to simply write about *something*. That's a recipe for disaster. Rather, they need to write about something *happening*. To find out if you fall into this camp, go through your story and assess what really *happens*—versus all the things you simply *show* and write *about*, all the things you are asking your reader to observe as opposed to *root for*, all the things your character experiences without an attachment to a dramatic core story question and an ensuing arc. If you struggle on these issues, you may be on to a major source of weakness. Diagnose that early, and your revision will be empowered in a significant and very necessary way.

A writer who doesn't know the true definition of a story can only hope to stumble upon, however intuitively, the complex sequence and forces of story in a way that really works.

And so I've developed a few iterations of questionnaires I use for stories in development, which I send to clients to dig into their stories and their knowledge of them. Filling out this questionnaire and then consulting with me is far more economical than hiring someone to read and evaluate an entire manuscript, and it shines a light on the very elements that will make a story compelling and emotionally resonant.

As I've said, I've done many hundreds of these story evaluations in the last few years, as well as dozens of full-manuscript evaluations. The numbers tell a story: Less than 10 percent of writers, even experienced writers, can answer the questions adequately. Many butcher the answers, transposing concept with premise, stating theme in the place of a core dramatic question, and mangling the intricacies of story structure to an extent that the available story physics don't stand a chance.

These writers may or may not have a solid story idea. But when it comes to the depth of understanding required, they just don't know. They either have to stick with it for years until their inner story sensibilities come to life … or until someone can show it to them.

I've included some of these answered questionnaires in the case studies in Part Four. There's a lot to notice, especially after you've been introduced to the empowering forces and structures of storytelling.

So when I say that writers just don't know, I say it with experienced authority. When agents tell you that ninety-five out of every one hundred stories that cross their desks aren't even close to the publishable level, they are saying the exact same thing.

What Jack Nicholson's character shouted in *A Few Good Men*—"You can't handle the truth!"—applies all too often.

Don't let that be you.

Begin with accepting the truth about your story, and then be honest about how much of it is alive in your writing mind.

That is the determining factor for everything you write. You can fake it once, you can get lucky once, but the odds of that are astronomically low, and next to zero if your goal is building a career.

You have to know what a story *is*.

Let me show you what that means.

WHEN AN AUTHOR DOESN'T GET IT

I recently sent the following response to answers to the questionnaire I use in my coaching work, and it was generic enough to be of value to any writer whose work has been rejected.

Read and learn from one author's feedback (used with permission), minus the pain of being that guy.

> To the author:
> This entire storytelling proposition consists of two realms of "raw material." One is the actual story premise itself; the other is execution. In both realms, the "outcome" is always determined by someone's opinion, though for execution this opinion is less negotiable and more easily predictable.
>
> It is on the first point where the room divides. One person's great story idea is another's yawn.
>
> Some love literary novels, others can't read them and prefer cozy mysteries or graphic horror stories or even erotica. Which of them is "wrong"? That's not the proper question, of course, but it seems to be such when a writer pitches a story, something she thinks is absolutely fascinating and rich in potential, and the responders (agent, editor, story coach, and ultimately readers) say, "Not my cup of tea," or "It didn't really grab me," or whatever.
>
> And thus, stories are accepted or rejected, successful or forgotten. Agents and editors "accept" stories all the time that they think will be appealing, and readers will stay away in droves because they don't agree. We haven't broken that code.
>
> In my case, in my role, I try not to gauge anything by "how I like it." Rather, I evaluate more like an engineer assessing a blueprint or a worksite for the raw beams of a structure and, ultimately, the viability of a finished structure.
>
> The engineer doesn't have to "like" a house or a building to deem it finished or worthy in terms of viability. That's not the job. It's not my job either. I'm here to look inside the story, at the core bones of it, and assess the nature of those building blocks. But in doing so, I can look at the specific, separate items and assess their strength, both

alone and in relation to the others (when they become a sum seeking to be a whole in excess of the parts).

Your story obviously really appeals to you.

I'm betting you've told others about it—"I want to tell the story of my hero and what happened to him during the war when the Russians took over his country, and there are some cool elements there, like a sailor picked up at sea, an affair, some nasty, paranoid Russians ..." Your listener goes, "Wow, that sounds like a great story! It'd make a great novel!"

The thing is, a great novel requires much more than a pile of cool elements.

From what I remember, your story is basically a true story, which immediately can be problematic because you feel the need to tell it "like it happened."

Yes, you certainly can write "what happened." And what happened is interesting, to some extent. But in a competitive market, other benchmarks and criteria apply. And that's where your story, as conceived and assembled, becomes suspect.

In my opinion, the story lacks the "physics" required to compete for a publisher. Those physics include:

- a compelling premise that becomes a story landscape for a hero's journey
- an escalating sense of dramatic tension arising from conflict
- strategic pacing
- an empathetic journey for a hero/protagonist that will cause the reader to root for his or her desired outcome (or problem solving), with an antagonist (villain or negative force) blocking the path
- a vicarious journey for readers (something they can't experience for themselves, which all historical novels seek to create)
- an effective narrative strategy

In other words, in summary, you lack a compelling plot.

The thing is, you can include all of these story physics and still come up short. But it is the sum that matters, and even though the parts may look good at first, when they combine they are not as compelling as they need to be.

It would be like someone writing a novel about the childhood of someone like, say, Cher. Cher is famous. Cher's fans will care. Nobody else will—unless and until the writer leverages the above list to generate a story they respond to emotionally.

In your case, your story has basic flaws, even prior to square one.

You lack a compelling hero. The hero isn't heroic (and even if he is heroic in the past, that doesn't matter, not a bit, in the foreground story). In fact, he's by nature not someone we root for, or even like (not a necessity by any means, but it can help if called for). This is because you don't give him a quest with a specific goal, something that has stakes.

He's trying to find the guy ... but why? Toward what end? You never tell us.

"But," you might say, "he does have a goal. He's trying to find MacGuffin (a character who becomes "the prize" and the source of stakes in the story; in *The Da Vinci Code* the MacGuffin was the Holy Grail, which turned out to be ... well, you already know that surprise ending)!"

Sure, but who is MacGuffin? We don't know. He's just a guy he picks up at sea. Then he disappears.

The bottom line: Nothing is riding on the hero finding him.

What if he does find him? What then? Nothing. The hero isn't going to save him; the hero isn't going to change everything. So there are no stakes attached to the hero finding MacGuffin.

Which boils your story down to: a guy finds a guy, and then loses the guy. We watch all that happen, without ever really knowing or, more importantly, feeling what this means, and thus, why we should care.

Everything depends on stakes.

Without them, a story becomes a "chronicle" or a documentary of a character's journey within the historical framework. It becomes a frame without a picture. Which is the case here: This story is about "the stuff that happens to the hero and the hero's wife," set on a tapestry of this political stage at that point in history.

But nothing happens that compels the reader to care. Your characters aren't known figures from history. And frankly, they aren't sympathetic in any way. So, if what they're doing isn't important, and who they are doesn't touch our hearts, why will we care?

Part of the problem, as I said, is how the book is written, as it sits now.

Your Part One needs a complete redesign, because you aren't setting up a compelling core story that launches at the First Plot Point.

You may argue with that. You may say you are setting up a core story, and that it is compelling. But we disagree on that point. It's not compelling because the hero has no skin in the MacGuffin game, and then when the Russians suspect he's somehow a spy, that's thin, hard to see or believe, and becomes a chase without a prize.

Because the hero isn't a spy. And the Russians' suspicion that he is has no basis other than paranoia.

In your synopsis you describe an ending in which neither the hero nor the hero's wife is actively, heroically involved. The hero never solves his problem, and the problem he has is, again, without depth or real meaning. The political stage becomes scenery. It is never about the hero seeking to save someone, or change something, or improve anything at all.

It's like a diary come to life. But the diary isn't dramatic enough, and has no substantive stakes, to become a novel that works.

Let me put it this way: The story of one guy who saves another guy, neither of whom made a lick of difference in the war, is not enough of a story. Thus, whatever happens to them (affairs, unfair pursuit, etc.) doesn't matter enough to get readers invested.

If, however, the hero is a guy who saves a very important guy—someone who ends up making a meaningful difference, or plays a key role in the outcome of what happened in those days in that place—then that is a story worth telling, from a commercial perspective.

You never position either player in the story relative to stakes. That's a deal killer.

Even then, though, the story is still about the hero's quest and heroism, not about his wife's affair and his abusive nature and his alcoholism, and his blind quest to find a guy about whom he knows nothing, with no noble intentions or vision for an outcome that will change anything, and then, doesn't end up achieving any of it, or anything at all.

That, in a nutshell, is what is wrong at the story premise level.

There is a long list of things that are wrong at the execution level, to the extent I think you need to come at this story—a better story—from a completely new and fresh narrative strategy. This will result in a much richer, faster, compelling Part One quartile that is not driven by backstory and meaningless character chit-chat and descriptions of setting and random memories and such.

All of this is despite your significant prose skills. You do write very well.

That said, you need a lot of work and practice on scene writing, which begins with a clear mission for each scene that connects to a compelling core story arc. If I'm correct when I suggest that the core story arc (what your Part One scenes seek to set up) is, in fact, less than compelling, then the scenes are already doomed. This is complicated by the fact that you overwrite them—and many of them don't serve the core story; they are side trips with the "diary" you are creating. The sum becomes something that calls for a closer look, with a view toward improving the core story (which means you need to change it), and finding a narrative strategy that better serves it, but focusing on the drama instead of the backstory or the subplots, which in the current version completely smother the intended "plot" itself.

When what your hero *does* matters, because *stakes* are involved that touch us emotionally and intellectually, then you'll be on point with this story.

Tough stuff, I know. The writer and I both hope that you benefit from this tough-love feedback. And, as you can see, there is a *lot* to know about your story before you can make it work.

Even if you're trying to retell a true story through the lens of a historical novel. A historical novel is fiction, which trumps what really happened. Unless you put "nonfiction" somewhere on the back cover, the principles of fiction will drive its effectiveness.

HOW TO TANK A JOB INTERVIEW

Sometimes when I present a writer with the observation that his story has no dramatic arc, too little tension, and thus, no real plot, he defends what he's done or disagrees outright. Again, we write what we write because we believe it is valid and powerful, and it still is in the writer's mind, even at the first hint that it actually isn't.

This is exactly like going on a job interview knowing that you don't possess the necessary skills or experience, and being told by the interviewer that your résumé doesn't match up to the job requirements.

And so you explain. You defend. You rationalize. Maybe you even plead for an exception.

Writers in this circumstance assure me that it'll all work out in the completed draft.

Go back to the interview analogy for a moment. You tell the interviewer that you're a fast learner, you're really smart, you never call in sick, and you *really* need the job. And you expect the interviewer to hire you over the throng of perfectly qualified applicants sitting in the waiting room.

You can guess how that will turn out. It never works, unless the interviewer is your uncle. And it rarely works in a story assessment process.

There are no benevolent uncles in publishing.

If you can't pitch it, if you don't know the sweet spots of how to pitch and hit them in your story as well, you can't really hope to write it well enough to work. That's just a fact. Because while an early draft may well be the place where you try to work out those fuzzy answers, it all needs to be crystal clear and artfully rendered in the draft you hope to sell.

Which brings us back to the need for revision, which, one would hope, is a step you take before showing it to agents and editors.

And so you are left with your own ability to assess what will work in the market, what will land you an agent or a publishing contract, or what will draw readers to it in the digital marketplace, using your story *sensibilities,* juxtaposed with whatever story criteria you accept as valid, for better or worse.

The most you can do is listen, and then launch a hunt for a higher story sensibility driven by the criteria and story physics that will make the novel or screenplay soar.

It's true: There is a market for anything.

So write what you want … right?

If you're an artist first, sure. If you're a professional, not so much. That's as crazy as the pilot deciding that instead of flying the planned route to Pittsburgh, she wants to fly to Atlanta today. Worse, she might fly halfway to Pittsburgh before turning south toward Atlanta, then thank you for flying with the airline today when you get off the plane all blurry-eyed and confused.

Writers do this. They rationalize exactly this, in just this fashion: *Because I'm free, I'm an artist, I can do this any way I want.* As absurd as the analogy is, it reflects a significant truth about why writers create doomed stories.

You are a *professional.* That changes everything.

Choose a better story.

Revision allows us to make a better choice about our stories, at the core level, which is the sweet spot.

What are your goals? I haven't met a writer yet who doesn't want his project to succeed, to even become a bestseller. So to be true to this goal, you absolutely *cannot* write anything you want. Every time we choose our stories we are placing a bet, and the principles of storytelling and a sense of the market define our odds for that bet. Sure, all ten people on the planet who want to live in that unthinkable house you want to build would trade places with you in a heartbeat. But does that qualify your plan as the basis for a major subdivision? Is it something a developer—the perfect analogy for a publisher in this example—would want to invest time and money in?

At the very least, you may finally understand why your story was rejected, and hopefully, what the specific areas of weakness are and where to find them.

Armed with this vast new awareness, a quiver of story development tools, and the cold-blooded clarity of criteria, the fate of your story is, now more than ever, truly in your hands.

PART FOUR

REDEMPTION

*Case Studies from the Real World
of Unpublished Stories*

13

THE DOCTOR WILL SEE YOU NOW

A quick word on how to get the most out of the case studies that follow: These projects are real. I haven't altered them other than to clean up the inherently sloppy nature of the back-and-forth exchange. At times I've included correspondence that shows the evolution of the writer's mind-set over this process, including a few that cushion the blow before they are hit with some sobering feedback.

The format for these case studies comes from my story-coaching work, which employs a story development questionnaire to define the writer's intentions and understanding of the story being worked on. In effect it is a pop quiz. If you don't know your whole and best core story, there is no hiding from that handicapping shortfall. If you don't understand the vocabulary of writing, if you don't know a concept from a theme, or a hook from a First Plot Point, you will be outed. Feedback to that effect stings, but it can be a real gift. It can save the writer a year of her life writing a draft that is already in a coma before it hits the page, or it can find and categorize story problems in existing drafts in the same way an MRI can find hidden leaks and growths.

These are real writers, all of whom have given permission to use their case studies here. That takes real courage, as I've selected these projects precisely because they illustrate gaps and shortfalls relative to an understanding of the principles and the necessary discipline of sticking to a core story. For the most part, these stories are early in their development, which is the best time to secure this type of feedback. One is for a finished manuscript, putting the writer in precisely the position you are in as someone who is facing a revision based on feedback.

You'll see, if you didn't already know, that writing a story at a professional level is not a casual pursuit. It is not something a hobbyist or someone totally new to fiction can hope to conquer easily. The truth is that it's a lot harder and more complex than it looks.

If you didn't know that already, you are about to find out.

One more thing: These examples actually demonstrate the norm rather than the lowest common denominator. After doing more than six hundred of these critiques in the past three years, and after several decades of story coaching on other fronts, I say this from personal experience. This is what happens. My hope is that, by ingesting these case studies, it may not happen to you.

THE BEST LEARNING OF ALL

As we move forward in our writing journey we gather knowledge and evolve our skills. Part of that process includes reading the published work of best-selling authors and, sometimes, the novels and screenplays of our peers. What we learn there depends on what we bring to that reading experience. If you are new to writing, then perhaps those published stories appear to be nearly seamless; they almost look *easy*. Sometimes, in the quiet of our hubris, we think we could do as well. And so we learn to duplicate what we see in successful works relative to storytelling craft.

But this can be like watching heart surgery from the operating room gallery and then trying to insert a valve into the heart of a loved one in your living room. Because it *looked* easy. It's a rather dark and absurd analogy, I grant you, but it's also apt. In the hands of a professional, the complex can appear symmetrically accessible. Chances are—actually, it's a certainty—your less-than-fully-enlightened eye doesn't capture all there is to learn when you read a best-selling novel or see a great film. Many of the details, principles, nuances, and creative moves disappear into the whole of the story.

The theory of spending ten thousand hours of apprenticeship to reach a professional level of excellence has no better testimony than in the field of writing fiction.

I contend that the more you understand about craft, the easier it is to identify both strengths and weaknesses in the work of others, which turns those works into better teaching tools.

And so, now that you've internalized this information and stand at the gate of storytelling enlightenment, you are about to enter an exciting new world, the realm of the principles screaming out to you from the pages of those same published novels in a way you've never been able to see and comprehend before. Your learning curve is about to go vertical, because this very experience—looking for and recognizing craft in the stories you consume, seeing how they did it, recognizing the principles in play—is the second most enlightening opportunity you'll ever know in your life as a writer.

This is assuming that you bring along your knowledge of craft as you review published stories. If you're still guessing or trying to prove these principles wrong, then you're on your own in recognizing the symmetrical and nuanced beauty of craft imbedded in the complex and distracting ambiance of a well-told story. It's like looking at an X-ray. It's almost impossible to see anything of importance until someone with a white coat points it out to you.

Hopefully you now have a white coat of your own to bring to the discussion.

You might be thinking, *So you said reading stories from this new context is the second most enlightening opportunity I'll have. Then what is the first, the best learning experience available?*

I was hoping you'd ask.

The only compromise in using published works as learning models is that any problems and miscues that may have existed during development, any departures and fumbling of the principles, have likely already been caught and remedied. Sure, you may find a typo or two in a published book, but we're talking story-level issues here, and those have been, for the most part, repaired. There's no case study of revision-in-waiting to be found in a finished David Baldacci novel or a Steven Zaillian script.

The richest learning experience awaits in reading the work of newer writers and their *unpublished* stories, stories that haven't yet reached up to grab the bar, even stories in development that expose what the writers aren't seeing, aren't getting, and may be tripping over as their words tumble into an abyss of their own digging.

When you read these stories and story plans with an enlightened eye, while embracing all the principles and criteria you have just consumed, this becomes the most affirming, illuminating, and clarifying learning experience of all. Because now you can see how it looks behind the scenes, on the bloody battlefield of story development, where chaos must be confronted and ignorance leading to seductive temptation must be conquered.

I'm betting you can relate to that.

And I'm trusting that, in these case studies, you'll quickly see what I saw as the guy *doing* the evaluation and giving the often difficult feedback.

Read and learn. Other than helping your writer friends or participating in a critique group, this may be the best opportunity you've ever had to experience a writing epiphany, for realization to manifest before your newly enlightened eyes.

Put on your story-coaching hat and see how a story looks from the outside, with a view toward understanding what went wrong from the inside.

14

CASE STUDY ONE

WHEN CONCEPT DISAPPEARS

The following analysis is focused on only the concept/premise level of story planning. The concept has potential (it nudges up against the criteria to become a *compelling* proposition), but notice how it seems to disappear, then quickly reappear before vanishing yet again, as the premise is explained. Concept should imbue premise with compelling energy, which doesn't happen here.

Notice, too, how the premise is never truly compelling. It's a bit soft and slightly vague. If feels pantsed, perhaps episodic, retrofitted to answer the question about premise. To be sure, it's too vague to cause an agent or editor to leap out of his seat waving a contract.

Premise is something you need to nail. It is the beating heart of a story. When you do nail it, it can be stated in a few short, glowing sentences. If it needs explaining, chances are it's not yet focused enough. The drama needs to leap from it; the stakes need to be clear.

As you read, can you clearly visualize the intended story from these answers? Does it sound like a novel you'd want to read?

GENRE: Thriller

What is the *dramatic concept* of your story? (Note: The seed or idea for a story and the *concept* of a story are usually *not* the same thing. Also, the theme is

rarely part of the answer here.) Try to define the concept in one sentence.

> In a modern-day urban city with a violent reputation, everyday citizens discover collective consciousness and collective memory as a way to combat corruption, racism, and violence through empathy and the ensuing solidarity. Some will use this ability to strengthen and heal themselves and the community, while others will seek to exploit and profit from this knowledge.

NOTES FROM LARRY: This is a killer concept if it's some sort of paranormal or supernatural phenomenon. If it is, this means your novel is not just a "thriller" but a "paranormal thriller."

If I'm taking you literally, though, there is an immediate disconnect between the expectations of a thriller and the description you've provided. In essence, what I'm reading—*if* this is not a speculative paranormal story—is that people come together, as one community, to fight darkness. This is more thematic than conceptual, and not a terribly strong (at a glance) conceptual story landscape.

Restate your *concept* in the form of a "What if?" question. (Example: *What if a major religion employs a secret sect of killers to keep its darkest secret secure?* Notice how that question doesn't speak to the theme; it speaks to plot and dramatic tension, which is the role of concept.)

> What if a form of collective consciousness allowed us to access our shared, collective memories? What if this ability was a path to combating corruption, racism, and violence? What if this kind of solidarity were used to create societal groupings to do good or to do evil?

NOTES FROM LARRY: Okay, it sounds like you're going down the speculative/paranormal path, which is good, because that's a more compelling proposition and thus a more compelling story landscape. It truly is a compelling "What if?" notion. (You will need to change your genre answer, though. The thriller genre has very tight expectations for agents, editors, and readers.)

One risk I see is the possibility that you will head down a sociological-study path rather than building the narrative around an unfolding dramatic spine. That would result in a theme-driven story, which is risky in any variation of the thriller genre. Your passion for the social issues shines through. Don't let it trump the story you need to tell.

The questions your current concept poses—what I'm asking now—are: How does this collective consciousness *happen*? What triggers it, and what happens then? And most of all (because you *need* this next part), how does it create a journey for a specific hero (a need, an opportunity, something that launches him or her down a dramatic path), and what *opposes* that hero's goal (a villain)?

That answer would be more conceptual than the one you have. People will be drawn to this proposition, but if it turns out that "one consciousness" manifests in town meetings and posters, that's not conceptual at all, and not something thriller readers will flock to.

The premise needs to point toward those answers. This *cannot* just be a story about "all the stuff that happens to these people once they get their heads together." One hero, one villain, one goal in between them—that's what you're after.

State the *premise* of your story. (Note: Concept and premise are different things, much like stone and statue. A statue can be made out of any number of things, including stone. One is substance, the other form.)

> The back channel politics of Oakland City Hall mean nothing to Juvenal, a struggling loner trying to change her life, until a chance encounter and new friendship with a sixteen-year-old boy draws her close to a ring of corrupt and dangerous adversaries. Along the way she discovers an old flame, a hidden talent, and a key that could unlock her fears. She'll need all the help she can get to lead her young friend out of a dead-end life path—and defeat the powerful political players who would do anything to protect their incomes, jobs, and reputations.

NOTES FROM LARRY: Be clear on this: Juvenal's story path is *her* vs. *city hall*, which means you must connect it to this other stuff—the old flame, the hidden talent, and the "key" to *that* quest. Otherwise it becomes a sideshow or a subplot. Be clear on the *core* story and stick to it. This is *not* a character study (you're in the wrong genre for that); this is about the *drama* of:

1. Juvenal's problem/need
2. what she does about it specifically
3. what she faces (villain) along the way
4. how she summons her inner hero to get it done

That's pretty much all there is; the other stuff will just slow this down.

You've talked *around* the primary purpose she has in this story (something about leading her young friend toward something, or away from something) without ever saying explicitly what that "something" is, other than it connects, somehow, to City Hall. This vagueness puts you at risk. The questions here connect to that something, and yet you never identify the core of the story. This reads more like book jacket copy, as if you're trying to "hook" the reader (me) into digging in, reading more (which absolutely isn't the purpose of stating the premise here). You haven't given me enough story, at its core, to analyze. Why save this friend? Why is the friend at risk?

This is like trying to describe *The Hunger Games* like this: "Katniss must overcome overwhelming odds to get back to her family." Well, sure … that's great for the book jacket, but for this purpose (analysis, with a view toward getting the story accepted), it totally misses the entire core of the plot, the action, the drama, the ethos. You've done the same thing here—you've skipped what is important, conceptually, at the core of the story. Read your answers again. You're circling the wagons without telling us what those wagons are.

This could be simply how you've answered the questions, or it could be symptomatic of a story problem at its core. With all good intentions, you may well be lacking relative to this critical story core. However you define this core, it needs to be conceptually compelling. It needs to give your hero something *specific* to *do*: a problem to solve, an opportunity to seize, a wrong to right. But again, even after I've asked for it, the answer is not here. Yet.

Notice, too, that your answers regarding premise have *absolutely no connection* to this notion of "connected minds" you introduced in the concept. It's gone, completely. That's a sign of a writer who isn't yet clear on the story she's writing. You might still be in the "search for story" phase, still drafting, without having landed on the highest, best, most compelling core story.

What *dramatic question* does this concept ask? (Example: Will Katniss survive the to-the-death contest into which she has been thrust?) The dramatic question is an extension—leading *toward* a story—of the premise itself.

> Will Juvie bring down the Oakland politicos, and in the process of showing her young friend how to change his life, discover that she knows how to change her own? Yes!

NOTES FROM LARRY: I like it. I don't quite love it yet, though … which could be rooted in how you've answered rather than in the story plan itself. This question doesn't seem to connect—yet—to the "one unified mind" concept, though. It's hard to see how that is being used in the story, how it colors the hero's journey in any way. Also, what is at *stake*? What is at risk, what threatens, what is the ticking clock (the essence of a thriller), and why her? You haven't even hinted yet at what the bad guys are up to.

What does your hero *need* or *want* in this story? What is his or her "story journey"? (Note: This is one that stumps a lot of writers, and yet, it's perhaps the *most important thing* you need to know about your story. For example, in a concept in which your hero needs to find the man that kidnapped his children, *don't* answer this question with something like this: "His primary need is to conquer the inner shyness and hesitation that

extends from his childhood as the son of a disapproving father." That may be the case, but it's *not* the answer to the question. For that particular concept, a good answer would be "The hero needs to find the location of the kidnappers soon because his daughter needs medicine and she'll die before he can scratch up the ransom money.")

> Juvie *needs* to obtain proof of the City Hall corruption that flows back onto Oakland's city streets *before* those two forces combine to neutralize her as a threat. She *wants* to rekindle her old flame, help her young buddy start a new path in life, and unstick herself from her own rut.

NOTES FROM LARRY: It is critical that you define what, specifically, the evil city hall villains are doing. Why? Because we need to care about it, be frightened or disgusted by it. Are they cheating on their expense accounts? That wouldn't move us. Are they blackmailing local businesses? That's stronger. Are they covering up corruption, working with the mafia, scamming the local tax coffers, running a prostitution ring? We need to know what, specifically, they are doing, and why Juvie cares about it. Is Juvie diving in simply as a good citizen, or is the corruption touching her life, or someone she knows and loves, directly? Before we can care about her quest in this story, we need to understand the stakes of it, the threat of it, and why she is moved to take action. We need to care. This is an emotional issue, and you need to manipulate the reader into emotional engagement through a better answer, one that would cause us to take action, too.

What is the primary *external* conflict/obstacle to that need or goal?

> The city hall official and the street-level crime lord (and, by extension, all of the street-level hoods involved) who will try to buy Juvie off and scare her to protect their scam. She knows that if they get desperate enough, they'll kill her.

NOTES FROM LARRY: You have some good conflicting elements here, but this answer doesn't yet seem to embrace any sort of paranormal consciousness, as promised in your concept.

Would corrupt city officials really "buy her off?" How does she threaten them? Moreover, how could a teenager logically and realistically pose a threat to these villains at all? How does she even know about it? It's not like teenagers, as a rule, are privy to the inner machinations of local politics, so what is Juvie's window into this dramatic setup? I fear this is too thin; you're not telling me what I need to know here. Is that because you don't realize how critical these answers are to the process, or that you truly don't know the answers at this point?

What are you asking your reader to *root* for in this story?

> The reader needs to root for Juvie to succeed in bringing down the city hall corruption ring and come out of it alive.

NOTES FROM LARRY: Good—once you show us *why* she needs to do this (stakes).

What is the First Plot Point in your story? (Note: This is the *most important moment* in your story, and it should connect directly to the concept and the dramatic question.)

> Lester and Juvie bond through a startling discovery: They can both recall the exact details of a time neither of them ever experienced, and it seems the two knew each other in that long-ago time. When Juvie decides to help Lester (age sixteen), she gets an introduction to Calvin, the crime lord. Just as Calvin gets threatening with Juvie, in walks Calvin's sister, Q—Juvie's old flame.

NOTES FROM LARRY: When you mention that Lester and Juvie can recall details of a time neither of them has experienced, is this the "one consciousness" thing? If so, good; it's here after all.

I'm not sure this First Plot Point will work, because it doesn't *obviously* launch Juvie down a new path. With more room to answer this, I'm confident you could explain how it does, but it's vague here. Meeting Calvin—or, perhaps, the reintroduction of the sister—needs to *change everything*, to swing the gates of the story wide open.

Also, remember that concept you pitched? The one about "collective consciousness"? I'm wondering where that went, and how it relates, even a little bit, to the story you're describing here. I fear it's disappeared entirely—which is not a good sign. Concept is important; it is the source of compelling energy for a story, the thing you've promised the reader. But I fear you've broken that promise, because the concept you pitched has almost nothing to do with the story you then tell.

At what point in your story does your First Plot Point occur? (Note: The optimal location is at the 20th to 25th percentile mark.)

> Ideally, the 20th percentile.

NOTES FROM LARRY: Yep, that's ideal. A lot of work to do, though, before this FPP can work.

Do you have another question about your story, concise and linked to the discussion of concept and premise, that you'd like to toss at me?

> I've been carrying this story around in my head for a while now, and I really want to get a tight, successful draft onto paper. I think I will have questions after I get your responses back. Thanks, Larry.

NOTES FROM LARRY: I hope this helps you move toward a more focused story. This has good potential, but after reading it, there is both confusion and lack of clarity on what this story is really about, even though, in asking these very questions, clarity is *precisely* what was called for. You wrote these answers, so my conclusion is that you are confused and unclear about this story. And that's a fatal blow.

Again, your answers often read too much like copy on the back of a paperback, and too little like a compelling pitch. The core story, the very thing that must be uncovered, the evil that must be stopped, remains vague. "Corruption" is not precise enough; there needs to be something specific that Juvie must prove and confront. An agent will say, "Fine, but what is the *story* about *dramatically*? Who wants what, and why? What opposes that (you dodged that one entirely)? What is at stake, and why? And what does your hero *do* about it?"

Lots to think about. I wish you well on next steps.

CASE STUDY TWO

WHEN THE BRAIN DIES,
THE REST FOLLOWS

This story is clearly from an author who has completed a draft. She has a response for everything (not necessarily a bad thing), which means she's defending rather than speculating on what could be better.

A story needs to work at its highest levels—concept, premise, dramatic question, character motivations, source of dramatic tension—before any of the details of execution matter. It's like evaluating the air-worthiness of an airplane rolling off the production line; if the engines don't start, you don't worry (yet) about the air conditioning. It simply won't fly.

That's what I felt about this story. It has potential, but I felt that it was an example of a "pantsed" story that wasn't built from the ground up, that it was pieced together one scene at a time, based on the author's sensibilities in a given moment. Unfortunately, in my opinion, the engines aren't starting. The whole thing needs a tune up.

CURRENT WORKING TITLE: *The Knowledge Gems*

GENRE: Fantasy

Which "voice" will you use: first-person past, first-person present, or third-person omniscient?

Third-person POV protagonist

What is the *dramatic concept* of your story? (Note: The seed or idea for a story and the concept of a story are usually *not* the same thing. Also, the theme is rarely part of the answer here.) Try to define the concept in one sentence.

> Hollity is an isolated city-state where honesty is treasured and citizens enjoy a good quality of life within a defined social structure. The talented few among the ruling elite are awarded a knowledge gem, a high honor, a "gift from the gods," which bestows a unique gift to each holder. Zero tolerance to crime means convicts are sent away to fight "bandits," a punishment from which no one returns. But Hollity is based on a lie: The gems are not god's gifts, they are mined by slaves on land conquered by Hollity eons ago, and the convicts are sent to protect the mines from rebels determined to take the mines back and destroy the city.

NOTES FROM LARRY: Could be interesting. But I have one question already: What's in it for the Hollity city fathers, the ruling class? All of this seems to be about protecting the mines, which implies (though you don't say it explicitly) that the mines yield a treasure of some sort. How does Hollity cash in on that treasure? Do they sell the gems somewhere? In such a futuristic fantasy world, gems are worthless, unless they are *not* worthless, which means that they have value, something worth protecting. Especially in this case, since you imply that the entire culture and the city itself depends on the mines ... but for what? Gems? That's fine, but what do they do with the gems that sustains the people, gives them power, or otherwise makes the gems the centerpiece of everything?

This is important, because the concept of the city (Hollity) has to make sense. Gems don't make sense as The Most Important Element of Life unless they are valuable for some reason. Do these gems have power? (And, if so, then *that* is the heart of the concept.) What is the "gift" you mention? And cities in reality never rely on gems; they rely on mining, perhaps, but only because they *sell* what has been mined.

In *The Hunger Games*, the games make sense because the president and the Capitol City cheeses use them to oppress the twelve districts. The games have a purpose in that regard, so the concept is legitimized. At a glance, your concept doesn't quite sell itself as logical. But this is easily fixed by making it logical and more clear in that regard.

Restate your concept in the form of a "What if?" question. (Example: *What if a major religion employs a secret sect of killers to keep its darkest secret secure?* Notice how that question doesn't speak to the theme; it speaks to plot and dramatic tension, which is the role of concept.)

> What if an idyllic city-state, which places high value on honesty, is built on a lie? What if its knowledge and wealth, which come from highly prized magical gems, are the fruits of slavery? What if rebels want to destroy the city and take back what they believe is theirs?

NOTES FROM LARRY: This is better, but I think you'll need to sell it. Magical gems? In what way? How does this give the city power and sustenance? And—putting on my cynic hat here—even if it's a lie, will the people really care? The key dramatic tension implied here—that the rebels are seeking to reclaim the mines—is interesting. But the lie itself … it's like how Europeans stole North America from the Indians … nobody cares about that anymore. (That's not to say that the Europeans stealing a continent from the Indians isn't a good story. Does your story spin on a similar culture-theft in this way?) So why will the people of Hollity care about this lie of how the mines were acquired?

I'll assume you'll sell this within the story—early—and I'll move forward under that assumption. That said, it's a little thin as described.

State the *premise* of your story. (Note: Concept and premise are different things, much like stone and statue. A statue can be made out of any number of things, including stone. One is substance, the other form.)

A talented student and herb healer, Fantine, striving for a prized knowledge gem, is unfairly failed in a crucial test by her teacher. When a gem is stolen, Fantine is wrongly convicted after being betrayed by her best friend, Berry (the teacher's daughter), and sentenced to fight the "bandits," a punishment assumed to be a death sentence.

NOTES FROM LARRY: This is a good opening hook and Part One set-up. But you need to bring these elements, which at a glance are separate threads, together in a single dramatic thread. What does her failing the test have to do with the betrayal of her friend, and what does either of those have to do with Fantine being sentenced to fight the bandits? Whether this works depends on how you tie all of it together. It won't work if it ends up being "here's a bunch of stuff that happens in this city."

Arriving at the far-away prison camp, she learns that her world is based on a lie: The gems are mined by slaves on land stolen by Hollity.

NOTES FROM LARRY: Again … she learns about the lie, but so what? There has to be stakes involved with that realization, a forthcoming mission that has purpose.

Finding herself caught in the middle of a rebel attack on the mines, Fantine gains incredible gem powers whilst saving the life of her lover. Against the odds, she makes it back to Hollity, determined to clear her name, bringing with her the dangerous truth about the real origin of the gems.

NOTES FROM LARRY: How does she obtain her "incredible gem powers"? This could seem contrived. You need to know how and why she, and not others, acquire "powers" from a gem, when everyone there is dealing with gems in their role as slave miners.

You're betting the story on the reader's buy-in. So far, it's thin ice, I think. How does having the gem clear her name, and, again, why and how is exposing the truth "dangerous"? That's critical to the premise. You have to *make* it dangerous, because a lie from the past is *not* inherently dangerous, even if it's shocking or scandalous.

Provide the synopsis for your story.

1. Fantine, a talented natural healer and class outsider, is unfairly failed on a test by a jealous teacher.

2. Scenes that introduce Fantine's talent and kindness, her unusual family background, the importance of the prized knowledge gems, and the social structure of Hollity, which unfairly discriminates against her.

3. After a gem is stolen, Fantine is wrongly accused and convicted, following a betrayal by her best friend, and is punished by being sent to the gem mines on a one-way journey.

4. On the way, she is betrayed by her new friend Dac and on arrival realizes that Hollity's power is based on a lie: The gems are mined by slaves on stolen land. After Dac comes back for her, she finds herself in the hands of rebels who want to reclaim the mines.

5. She unlocks a gem and is bestowed with energy healing, but not only that, she can use it in combination with the herb healing. This is unique, but the rebels take the gem away to deny her the chance to bond to its powers.

6. The rebels renege on their promise to free Fantine and Dac after she heals the rebel leader. They drag Dac on a suicide mission to bomb the mines.

7. Dac makes it back to her but is dying of his injuries. Fantine discovers she doesn't need the gem to do energy healing; she has bonded to it immediately. This is unheard of.

8. She escapes with Dac and heads to Hollity not only to clear her name but to save the city, knowing she could face execution on return. It's a race against time to get there before the rebels do. During a rebel attack she discovers she can unlock every gem and her powers deter the rebels. She is truly unique and special.

9. She gets home, finds out the truth about the original betrayal, is pardoned, and is the only one who can save the city from the rebel assault.

What *dramatic question* does this concept ask? (Example: Will Katniss survive the to-the-death contest into which she has been thrust?) This is often an extension—leading *toward* a story—from the dramatic question itself.

> Against the odds, and with her life in constant peril, can Fantine get home to find out why Berry betrayed her and clear her name?

NOTES FROM LARRY: The hero's motivations are critical to making a story work. Fantine wants to clear her name. Fine, but why? And why will we care? It seems a little self-focused for her; she's not "saving" anybody, it's all about her image in the community. This isn't all that dramatic relative to stakes. What is heroic about her quest—the need to prove herself innocent? Every convict in every prison hopes to prove themselves innocent … and there's nothing inherently heroic in doing so, even if they *are* innocent. The stakes need to be higher, playing for something bigger than herself.

This reveal needs to connect to the big picture (which is still a little unclear), and there needs to be stakes involved, something beyond her own good name. Her innocence, or not, is a small story compared to her doing something (like Katniss is doing in The Hunger Games series) that benefits the entire population, or even the oppressed part of it.

> Through her ordeals she uncovers beautiful truths about herself and ugly truths about her homeland and has to learn to trust again and also to forgive.

NOTES FROM LARRY: These truths, beautiful or otherwise, don't matter unless they *change* something, and unless the change is opposed by the people in power, causing them to try to stop her. What she learns about herself is secondary; a plot about self-discovery is weak because there are no stakes involved. There need to be big stakes in a story like this. This isn't a character study; it needs to be *big*, a story about a girl becoming a hero. Learning about one's self is not the stuff of heroics in stories. It should be bigger.

What is the *external* source of *conflict* your hero must face? (Note: If this answer doesn't match the previous question, we need to talk.)

> Fantine is sent away before she can discover why she was betrayed and clear her name. Before she can find her way home, she must survive cruel guards at the prison camp and violent rebels who drag her into their plot to take back the mines.

NOTES FROM LARRY: Major caution here: It sounds like you have no primary villain in the story. In fact, it sounds like it will be episodic, "the adventures of Fantine as she struggles to get back to the city ..." but to do *what*, exactly?

As in *The Hunger Games*, you need a villain, a face for whatever blocks the hero's path (it's the president in that case; it boils down to Katniss vs. the president). In your story, what does it boil down to, confrontation-wise: Fantine vs. ... who? And why?

What does your hero *need* or *want* in this story? What is his or her "story journey"? (Note: This is one that stumps a lot of writers, and yet, it's perhaps the *most important thing* you need to know about your story. For example, in a concept in which your hero needs to find the man that kidnapped his children, *don't* answer this question with something like this: "His primary need is to conquer the inner shyness and hesitation that extends from his childhood as the son of a disapproving father." That may be the case, but it's *not* the answer to the question. For that particular concept, a good answer would be "The hero needs to find the location of the kidnappers soon because his daughter needs medicine and she'll die before he can scratch up the ransom money.")

Fantine needs to survive her punishment and the rebel attack and get home to discover why she was betrayed and clear her name.

NOTES FROM LARRY: My opinion: This is too thin. Why would the reader *care* about Fantine clearing her name? What are we rooting for? What are the stakes in doing so? She clears her name, and then what? Who benefits? She should be playing for more than just clearing her name. Of course she's earning her continued freedom—and that's good—but it's still not enough. With this setup, it's all about her. It's self-focused, whereas great heroes are fighting for the good of others, the good of all. You haven't put Fantine into that position with this setup—it's too small. You need to give her a bigger, darker, more important game to play, with stakes that extend beyond herself.

Also, the core of your concept was those magical gems. But they've completely disappeared for the story you're telling here. In fact, there is no high-level corruption going on at all—it's all about her. It would work better if it ends up being about a bigger picture.

What dramatic question does this present? (Example: "Will the hero get the girl in the end, despite XYZ?")

Will Fantine survive and return to clear her name?

NOTES FROM LARRY: This could be stronger. Why will the reader *care* that she succeeds? What are the stakes of this, beyond her own well-being?

How will she be received if/when she gets back, given that the leaders of Hollity are led to believe she's a traitor on the side of the rebels, and given that she can expose the lie of the gems and given that the gem powers she gains are far and above those of even the leader of Hollity?

NOTES FROM LARRY: Again, what is the *risk* to the leaders of Fantine exposing the lie?

Why is she the only one with access to this level of power? This last part needs to be explained, and it needs to be logical. Be careful of contrivances in a story like this; everything needs to make sense.

What are you asking your reader to *root* for in this story?

> To root for Fantine to clear her name because she is neither guilty nor a traitor.

NOTES FROM LARRY: That's not enough; we need a much bigger, stronger reason to root for her. What are the stakes, the upside, the consequences, of her clearing her name? Why should we root for that?

> Readers will see she is talented and adored by many because throughout the story she selflessly uses her herb healing to help even those who act against her, including the camp commandant, the rebel leader, and fellow prisoner Jineen, who betrays her because she is jealous of her relationship with fellow prisoner Dac. The reader will ache to know why Berry betrayed her.

NOTES FROM LARRY: I disagree. It's too thin. Leaning into soap opera, I fear. I think, based on this, that you are still in the "search for story" phase, that you haven't found or defined a story that is strong enough yet. The fix is a *bigger* story with stronger stakes, and a logical reason that Fantine becomes a player, probably the lynchpin player, in saving the rebels and the oppressed from the leaders. How does "the lie" even matter? What happens if that is exposed (at a glance, there are no consequences to this).

The story, as is, is not broken, per se; it just isn't strong enough, in my opinion. Use *The Hunger Games* and Katniss (or any other story in the dystopian genre) as a model, and you'll see that these heroes are all playing for much larger, darker, and more urgent stakes than Fantine is engaged with, something for The Greater Good, beyond her own innocence.

What opposes the hero (the exterior antagonist) in the pursuit of this goal?

> Before the First Plot Point, the teacher who accuses her, and Berry (the daughter of the teacher) who betrays her. After, the rebels who use her to further their cause and then renege on their promise to

free her; the ambitious camp guard Garin, who wants the commandant's job; and the council, who wrongly convicted her and who, upon her return, do not at first believe her side of the story. Also, the constant threat to her life after the First Plot Point.

NOTES FROM LARRY: The story would benefit from a singular villain, the face of that which opposes her (and opposes her on a stronger, more urgent quest than the one you've given her). What you have is episodic, a series of minor antagonists who simply go away, leaving us with "the adventures of Fantine" as she travels this story road. While you could *make* it work, it isn't strong enough at its core to work at a higher level.

What are the goals, motivations, and/or rationale of the exterior antagonist?

> The teacher is jealous because her daughter Berry is not talented.

NOTES FROM LARRY: This is the setup of the story. The teacher isn't the villain *until and unless* that teacher is the one who emerges as the primary antagonist in Fantine's story quest over the arc of the *whole* story. This isn't the case here.

There was a really bad TV movie with a similar villain dynamic: The mother of a girl who is competing for a place on a cheerleading squad sabotages, and then tries to kill, one of the more talented girls competing for a spot. Notice this wasn't based on a novel. In fact, it's really thin villain motivation, bordering on the absurd.

> She looks down on Fantine because she is mixed class, the daughter of an elite father and a Workfolk (lower-class) mother. Fantine gets her herb healing talent from her mother, a skill looked down upon by the elite who use gem healing. It later transpires that Fantine's father passed the teacher over to marry her mother, and although the teacher went on to marry a high elite council member, she never got over the rejection.

NOTES FROM LARRY: This is all backstory and setup ... but not the villain you need.

Camp guard Garin takes a disliking to Fantine when he blames her for the escape of Dac and more so when she gains favor from the Commandant, the drunken brother of the leader of the council, by healing him.

NOTES FROM LARRY: This guy is only a villain *until* she breaks out and arrives in the city, where a villain isn't present at all. This, alone, exposes the story as too episodic.

Your answers describe relationships and nuances well into the story, when the problem with this resides at the highest levels of the story, rendering these answers moot. What is the big-picture dramatic story here? That's simply not clear, and less than compelling, in your answer.

The council believes she is a criminal and a traitor, and upon her return is afraid of her powers and that she can expose the lie their society is based upon.

NOTES FROM LARRY: A "council" isn't a good villain. You need *one* person who has reasons to stop her and gives us *someone* (not a council) to root *against*. What does the council have to lose? How does Fantine threaten them? That seems vague, yet it's critical to making this work.

What is at *stake* for the hero relative to attaining (or not attaining) the goal (which can be stated as survival, the attainment of something, the avoidance of something, the discovery of something, and so on)?

Survival, not getting back to clear her name, not knowing why she was set up and betrayed.

NOTES FROM LARRY: Too small. Too self-focused. She's not enough of a hero. Why will we care? She needs a higher purpose, something that is truly heroic, such as fighting to save the oppressed and *changing* the city itself. She gets her record cleared … so what? That's too small a story.

Notice she's not out to stop the bad guys or to bring them to justice. It's all about her. She's not heroic enough, and her quest isn't compelling enough, because the stakes are too inward, and not something that will motivate the reader to empathize.

Virtually everything you promised in your concept, whatever was conceptual, is completely gone now. There are no more magical gems from the gods, no more political fraud to be exposed; it's just your hero trying to clear her name. The story has jumped lanes, from an unclear and illogical lane into a thin and narrowly focused lane, now void of potential heroism, rendered less than compellingly dramatic because of its episodic nature.

Moreover, it's chaotic. The focus seems to jump from arena to arena, without an overriding, compelling dramatic question with stakes that make us care. That's what's missing here. When you throw in the chaos, the whole thing is destined for a rejection slip.

You need a stronger concept and premise, at square one, before this will work as you hope it will. An agent will tell you the same thing: This is too small. There aren't enough strong stakes in play. It's all over the place, and it has no dramatic focus that connects to the concept you have pitched.

Until that happens—a stronger story, and a much more dramatic, stakes-driven story arc—the remaining answers don't matter in context to this feedback. They are describing a story that is too small and won't work at the level you need, the level required to land an agent or a publisher, or, if you self-publish, a significant readership.

The problem, and the fix, is at the core level of concept and premise. This isn't big enough. You need a singular villain, opposing a much more meaningful, urgent, and heroic quest for your hero than what you have in place now. Fantine needs to "fix" something, expose bad guys, save the community. None of that is in play as described.

When you get that, everything in the story will change. The Part One setup will change, because you'll be setting up something else, something bigger (the big picture). The First Plot Point will change because that newer, bigger, better story will give your hero a larger, more consequential quest, against a stronger, singular antagonistic villain. Thus, the other story milestones change in context to all that.

I'm sorry if this sounds like a "back to the drawing board" conclusion, but that's precisely my call here. You're not done crafting a story that is deep enough, that gives us a protagonist with an empathic-enough quest, something with much stronger stakes attached, and, thus, much stronger drama along the way, against a much stronger singular villain who blocks her path precisely because the city itself will crumble if she succeeds.

In your current story, once she has her good name back, and once "the lie" is exposed, nothing changes for the city or anyone else. It's too small. My job here, the highest calling of this process, is to identify any potential issues that will hold a story back, as well as evaluate the blueprint, which depends on a solid concept and premise as its basis. When those are thin, the structural stuff becomes a moot point.

You do show a good comprehension of many of the basics here, including structure. But I think you've settled on a story too soon, a story that doesn't deliver something amazing and fresh and knock-an-agent-out-of-the-chair compelling—because it has some holes and some thin ice, as I've described.

I hope, once the sting of this subsides, that you find this feedback exciting, because now you know what the need is, and the challenge is clear. As is, the story isn't horrible, but it's just not strong enough. Again, that's my opinion.

Thanks for the chance to chip in. I wish you the best with this going forward.

CASE STUDY THREE

EVEN A WINNER RAISES YELLOW FLAGS

The cover memo I sent to this writer with her feedback, which appears below, tells you everything you need to know before reading this case study: the issues, the missteps, the virtues. Learn from these issues, and look for the contextual connections between them.

The news isn't always bad. Yet a nod in the direction of improvement is always a good thing in the early stages of story development—even if you develop that clarity for yourself, from your growing story sensibility. That's the ultimate goal: to be able to spot potential weakness before the story leaves your hard drive.

Even writers with promising stories don't quite grasp the true nature and function of premise. There is nothing more critical to a story. You are about to see that situation here, in what is a really solid story proposition. See what it looks like. Learn to recognize it in your own work.

LARRY'S COVER MEMO TO THE AUTHOR

Hi _____,

Here you go. I *love* your story. I think it has huge potential.

I give you a hard time in your statement(s) of concept, premise, and theme. You are off the mark in your understanding of all three terms. I think you need a crash course on those elements and their subtleties, as they are important to the writing itself.

My notes on the story sequence are prompts and yellow flags. You do have a nice dramatic arc in play, and I think I've given you some saves and added some additional value.

I make a drastic suggestion in my closing comments, which alters everything, including how you view the story. It's part of my urging to think *bigger* with this. Your narrative strategy, as is, is self-limiting, for reasons I explain in my responses.

Thanks for letting me play here. I wish you great success. You have the raw stuff to make it happen with the bones of this story. I hope you'll go for it!

Larry

Current working title:

The Secret Daughter

NOTES FROM LARRY: I like the title. That's an important element. This catches my eye.

Genre:

Historical fiction with a romantic element. Possibly it's historical romance, but I am perplexed and confused about this. I have written a story about real historical figures, which screams historical fiction, but two of my critique partners (who are romance writers) say that it is a romance. One of my critique partners (who writes mainstream women's fiction) says it could be either.

NOTES FROM LARRY: Historical fiction is one of the toughest genres to pull off. Also note that it's often a *very* risky proposition to write a story about real historical figures. It sounds like you're leaning more into historical. That said, it's perfectly fine to write a historical romance. That seems to be where this story lands.

As you will see below, my genre dilemma is driving me batty because if I just knew where it belonged I would probably know what my POV voices should be!

NOTES FROM LARRY: Don't sweat genre. Write the book you want to write, and see what happens. If it works, an agent will see it, and she'll find a place for it.

Which "voice" will you use: first-person past, first-person present, or third-person omniscient?

> My current/initial draft is in multiple third-person points of view (heroine, hero, antagonist).
>
> Problems: The concept of my story aligns with historical fiction, but there is also a romantic subplot that ends with a happily ever after. So I have a heroine POV, the love interest/sworn protector (hero) POV, and an antagonist POV. The main journey is the heroine's (but the love interest also has a fully fleshed-out arc, including plot points). I have toyed with the idea of making her POV first person and the love interest and antagonist third person. But is this too difficult for an unpublished author to make work?

NOTES FROM LARRY: I don't know about *difficult*; that depends on the writer, what he or she considers to be difficult. The more important question is: Which mixture of voice works best for this book? I love novels that offer mixed POV, and usually the protagonist is in first person (*The Great Gatsby* being an exception), and the other POV, that of the catalytic character, is told in third (because it often shows exposition from behind the curtain of the protagonist's POV).

I have a nit with the romance writer lingo. Books have a *hero*, which is the protagonist. This is the case with any genre. The male character, often an antagonist, is *not* the "hero" and the female character, if she is indeed the protagonist, is *not* the "heroine." Those labels work only in one niche—the romance world. If you're attempting to cross genre to any extent, then your protagonist (the woman, in this case) is the hero, and the guy is either a supporting character, a love interest, or the antagonist. That's how it's spoken of and thought of outside of romance, which is the broader market here.

For purposes of this analysis, and to avoid confusion, when I refer to your "hero" I'm talking about your *protagonist*, which in this case is your female lead character.

Should I play it safe by keeping her POV in third person?

NOTES FROM LARRY: Safe? Where'd you get *that*? Is it "safe" to choose a less effective narrative strategy? Absolutely not. The safest strategy is the *best* strategy, and if the story allows your hero's voice to be heard in a more intimate and revealing (and entertaining, because she'll have a "voice") context, then give her to us in *first* person.

> Or does third person for my heroine and my hero scream the romance genre, which, from experience and what I can tell, might and probably is not where my story fits.

NOTES FROM LARRY: Like I said, forget about genre. Aim higher. Write the novel, and tell your story. Genre is limiting. Huge breakout hits almost always cross genre lines.

Restate your *concept* in the form of a "What if?" question. (Example: *What if a major religion employs a secret sect of killers to keep its darkest secret secure?* Notice how that question doesn't speak to the theme; it speaks to plot and dramatic tension, which is the role of concept.)

> What if Julius Caesar had a secret, illegitimate daughter and the language in his will made it possible for her unborn child to be his adopted heir? What if she (Tertia) was the wife of one of his assassins (Cassius) and the sister of another (Brutus)?

NOTES FROM LARRY: Fabulous concept. And it's way *more* than a romance novel. Please, please, please (with much respect to your romance-writing friends) get over the romance vocabulary and limitations. Write a killer historical under this concept, driven by a sweeping love story.

This is *not* a romance. That concept sets the stage for a wonderful mainstream romantic historical novel.

> As an aside, Tertia was a real historical person, though not much is known about her except that she was Cassius's wife and Brutus's

sister, and that her mother had an affair with Caesar. I took it upon myself to give her a story!

I also have a story concept for the love interest (Alex).

NOTES FROM LARRY: To clarify, the "concept" is the foundation of the book and the story—not of a character. Characters don't have different concepts within a story (and thus you can't have a "story concept" for Alex). That won't work. Characters interact on the same conceptual story landscape.

Maybe you simply have a subplot. But Alex doesn't have his "own concept"; that's sideways thinking and incorrect labeling.

What if Julius Caesar knew he was going to die, knew who the conspirators were, and wanted to protect his secret, illegitimate daughter if something happened to him?

As an aside, Alex is purely fictional.

NOTES FROM LARRY: This is totally part of—a hierarchical progression of—the *same* concept.

You have *one* concept here, and it's good. It doesn't matter that Alex's story is fictional and that Tertia's is based on supposed fact. The truth is, Tertia's story, as it unfolds here, will be mostly made up by you anyway. Any differentiation on your part could really compromise the storytelling.

State the *premise* of your story. (Note: Concept and premise are different things, much like stone and statue. A statue can be made out of any number of things, including stone. One is substance, the other form.)

NOTES FROM LARRY: Before I respond to your answer in full, I should clarify that a story has *one* premise. Characters don't have a premise; they experience an "arc" over a single premise (albeit perhaps with different facets and points of view), which drives the story. Premise describes the source of dramatic tension, in other words, a *plot*.

Did you read *The Help*? There are three main characters. Are there three concepts, and three premises? If you think so, allow me to change your mind.

What you are about to offer here are three character arcs. It is *critical* that they intersect, that they become parts, facets, of the *same* story, under the *same* premise. Three premises ... no way. One story, with three characters ... that's what your story is, what you should shoot for, and how, beginning now, you need to think of it and describe it.

> Tertia's story premise: When Julius Caesar's illegitimate daughter discovers her unborn child could be his adopted heir, she reveals her true identity, despite knowing that her family might disown her, to secure the inheritance so that she and her baby will have the means and the power to be free of her abusive husband.

> Alex's story premise: When Julius Caesar's bodyguard, who is sworn to protect Caesar's illegitimate daughter, witnesses her being beaten by her abusive husband, he puts her in hiding, despite finding himself unsuitably attracted to her, to safeguard her from those who want to harm her.

NOTES FROM LARRY: See my notes prior to your answer, and make sure you fully understand the definition of premise. That said, this all sounds terrific so far. The story is just fine, even if you need to rethink your understanding of premise. Premise is one of the most important elements of a good story, and it begins by knowing what a premise *is*.

> Both story premises transform the story concepts into inciting incidents for each character and each character is given an external goal that has stakes, an external conflict and a motivation.

NOTES FROM LARRY: This is making me crazy. You have wonderful story on your hands. But be clear: You need *one* concept, *one* premise, *one* hero, and several *other* characters that influence, pressure, challenge, support, and so on.

> I plan on answering the rest of the questions for my main plot—
> Tertia's story.

NOTES FROM LARRY: Again, this needs to be about the *one singular story* that all of these character arcs represent. I'm hooked—I want to know what happens. And what happens will include the involvement of all the major players.

What is the core dramatic thread of the story, as introduced in your statement of premise?

Freedom.

NOTES FROM LARRY: Sorry, but this is the *theme* of the story. You must understand the difference between concept, premise, and theme. They are three very different (but related and dependent) story elements.

A core dramatic thread, what this question asks for, is the thing the hero must *do* (not what she *wants*) to achieve her goal (*that* is what she wants), and the nature of whatever stands in her way (which is *essential*) and what is at stake.

In other words, it is the *plot* of a story. "Freedom" is not a plot. It is a theme.

Unfortunately, you've just blown the most important question of all. Better stated, you've just demonstrated that you don't understand the most important principle in all of fiction writing. You cannot write the book well enough to secure a contract without an understanding the most important aspect of the entire story: What is your dramatic premise, the core dramatic spine that emerges from it, and the core dramatic question it poses, which will elicit reader empathy by giving the hero something important to do, with significant stakes in play, and someone or something blocking her path in that quest?

"Freedom" is an outcome. It is not the story, and it is not a dramatic question.

I recommend you immerse yourself in 101-level craft until you get clarity on these principles. You have a strong story concept and, with some tweaking, a strong premise on your hands, but you have to be up to the task. Make sure you are—the principles that will inform your writing aren't something you can fake or guess at. You need more fundamental craft before you begin to write this story. That's my opinion, based on these answers.

What is the *external* source of *conflict* your hero must face? (Note: If this answer doesn't match the previous question, we need to talk.)

> Her abusive husband (Cassius).

NOTES FROM LARRY: This is fine. But he has to continually *do something* specific to become her foe, her nemesis. It is her vs. him in this story.

Not to be too picky with this … yes, the external conflict is Cassius, but the *reason* he opposes her is the primary conflict. Which means that you have to show Cassius's motivations and stakes, what *he* has to win or lose, so we understand the lengths he'll go to attain what he needs.

What does your hero *need* or *want* in this story? What is his or her "story journey"? (Note: This is one that stumps a lot of writers, and yet, it's perhaps the *most important thing* you need to know about your story. For example, in a concept in which your hero needs to find the man that kidnapped his children, *don't* answer this question with something like this: "His primary need is to conquer the inner shyness and hesitation that extends from his childhood as the son of a disapproving father." That may be the case, but it's *not* the answer to the question. For that particular concept, a good answer would be "The hero needs to find the location of the kidnappers soon because his daughter needs medicine and she'll die before he can scratch up the ransom money.")

> To be free of her husband.

NOTES FROM LARRY: Yes, but that's only part of her goal. She wants the inheritance, and she wants to take care of her child as well. She needs to be free of him in order to do those things.

What is the primary *external* conflict/obstacle to that need or goal?

Will Tertia free herself from her husband?

NOTES FROM LARRY: Well, now you've answered with a dramatic question. You actually haven't answered the posed question at all. You imply that her husband is that obstacle, but that may not be true; it may be too simplistic. This question asks for a villain, yet your answer is her *need*.

My earlier suggestion to gain a better 101-level understanding before you begin to write? Every answer you give demonstrates how badly you need to elevate your knowledge in that realm.

What are you asking your reader to *root* for in this story?

For Tertia to be free from her husband and for Tertia to be with the love interest.

NOTES FROM LARRY: Good stuff. It's easy to root for that.

Why should they root for it?

Because her husband abuses her. Because her husband killed her father. Because the love interest believes in her and, unlike her husband, sees her for who she is or who she should be.

NOTES FROM LARRY: There is a built-in curiosity factor here. How could she possibly defeat her powerful husband on this issue? Doesn't he rule the courts that she'll need in order to prove the will is valid? The reader will not only root for her on a personal level, but they'll stick around to see how she plans to pull this off. I hope you have a credible, visceral *means* by which she will attain this goal.

WHAT OPPOSES THE HERO (THE EXTERIOR ANTAGONIST) IN THE PURSUIT OF THIS GOAL?

Her husband, Cassius.

What are the goals/motivations/rationale of that antagonist?

Cassius wants to restore Rome's Republic from Caesar's supposed tyrannical rule and therefore achieve his own political greatness. To do this he needs to maintain his marriage with Brutus's sister to not only ensure Brutus as a colleague/political partner but also to keep Tertia's landed dowry, which provides him the income that he needs for his political aspirations.

At first, Cassius is appalled that his wife is Caesar's daughter, but he then realizes that it will help him and at the same time be gleefully ironic. Not only has he killed Julius Caesar, but now Cassius's child can inherit Caesar's wealth, which Cassius can use to further his political agendas.

NOTES FROM LARRY: This is a little confusing. It seems Cassius and Tertia share the same goal—that the kid inherits Caesars' fortune. So where is the conflict? You need to sort this out and draw clear battle lines in the story.

What is *at stake* for the hero relative to attaining (or not attaining) the goal (which can be stated as survival, the attainment of something, the avoidance of something, the discovery of something, and so on)?

Losing her family, more specifically her mother and her aunt—the people she loves.

NOTES FROM LARRY: This implies that Cassius, in trying to gain control over her son's inherited fortune, will somehow separate her from her son. That means more is going on, and that the marriage is over as well. Again, this needs to be clear, because at first glance, it isn't.

What inner demons will plague your hero through this story?

Tertia grew up in the shadow of her siblings, leaving her convinced that nothing she ever did was good enough or important enough to deserve recognition. She wed Cassius to secure a political alliance for her brother Brutus, believing her marriage to Cassius would define her worth. But the abuse Cassius unleashes on her continues with no end.

NOTES FROM LARRY: Good. How do you plan on using this in your story?

What is your hero's world view, goals, values, problems, etc. *prior* to the First Plot Point? (This is where the story-specific quest, in context to obstacles and stakes, is launched or imbued with meaning. Sometimes the FPP is a moment that heightens or changes something the hero is already engaged with.)

The story begins at Caesar's funeral (public cremation), where the reader is shown that Tertia hadn't known who her real father was until he was already dead. Since there is a threat that the city mob (Caesar's supporters) might try to raid the homes of the assassins, she goes back to her marital home to get her most precious possessions before it is too late. There she has a confrontation with Cassius, where it is revealed to him that she is Caesar's daughter and she is pregnant. Her protector/love interest Alex saves her from a severe beating, and he puts her into hiding at his sister's home.

NOTES FROM LARRY: Good stuff. Very dramatic, a great hook.

How will the hero's world view, goals, values, problems, etc. build reader empathy prior to the arrival of the First Plot Point?

Alex's sister lives in a working-class neighborhood. Tertia is a fish out of water here. Her patrician background does not help her fit in, and she feels even more worthless because she does not have a skill set to help his sister in her day-to-day activities.

NOTES FROM LARRY: Well, compared to her bigger problems, this is pretty small potatoes. This is *not* what the story is about (how she fits in while staying with Alex's sister); the story is *way* bigger than that. We need to understand and empathize with her *big-picture* situation: Her husband wants to beat her and kill her, and perhaps take her son from her so he can control the inheritance. We will feel empathy for *that*, not how she fits in with the local book club in the new neighborhood.

Keep in mind what the *core story* is. Don't let little details (which are the basis for your answer here) overcome and trump the main story arc and the primary dramatic question.

"Will she fit in with Alex's sister's friends?" is *not* the core dramatic question of this novel. Not by a long shot.

What is the theme(s) of your story (the subtext)? What issues are at hand in your story? (State this in less than 100 words, please.)

> Your worth in the world is measured by the value you place on yourself.

NOTES FROM LARRY: That's pretty specific. It's fine, but it seems the themes are greed, moral corruption, and narcissism. Also, where did "freedom" end up relative to the issue of theme? Earlier you said the story is all *about* theme (when you incorrectly labeled it the core dramatic question), but it doesn't appear in this answer.

What is the First Plot Point in your story? (Note: This is the *most important moment* in your story, and it should connect directly to the concept and the dramatic question.)

> Tertia reveals her identity to Mark Antony (the acting head magistrate of Rome) so he will help her secure Caesar's inheritance for

her unborn child despite her family disowning her. The inheritance needs to be approved by the Senate due to Caesar's posthumous adoption.

NOTES FROM LARRY: At a glance, this is a good FPP. How does she *prove* that the child she carries is Caesar's grandchild? That seems critical. She's the sister of the assassin, which already puts her credibility in question. It seems like she'd need a letter from Caesar himself confirming this. Just pitching it to Mark Antony may not be enough, *especially* since Mark Antony has his own plans for the inheritance. He wouldn't just say, "Oh, you're the mother of Caesar's heir? Gosh darn, okay, if you say so … I guess I'll have to abandon my evil agenda."

How does this spin the story in a new direction? In what way does this begin or alter your hero's journey? How does the FPP put *stakes* and *conflict* into play that weren't readily apparent in the Part One scenes?

The arena of antagonists widens because her true identity is now known.

NOTES FROM LARRY: How does she prove her identity, other than claiming it?

Tertia becomes the MacGuffin—she has what everyone wants (the heir). Mark Antony felt that he should have been the heir. The heir-apparent, Octavius, thinks he's the heir. It is also the first time she stands up for herself and acts.

NOTES FROM LARRY: Here's where it isn't clear. They *want* her, because she has what they *really* want … but what does that mean? They want her *dead*? They want her to marry [insert name]? What do they really hope for? Seems like they "want her out of the way" rather that simply wanting her.

These motivations on the part of the various antagonists need to be *clear* and *scary*.

It's a good plot point, if it's credible. Tertia simply standing up for herself isn't enough. She needs to *prove* it, and when she does, now the game is really "on." We need to *see* her standing up for herself, and there need to be consequences that launch her down the story path.

Here's another issue: How does this FPP alter her path, create a quest, and launch the dramatic path toward confrontation with the antagonist(s)? That's not quite clear yet.

At what point in your story does your First Plot Point occur? (Note: The optimal location is at the 20th to 25th percentile mark.)

> At the 23 percent mark.

NOTES FROM LARRY: This is ideal.

What happens in your Part Two scenes? How does this illustrate a *response* (the contextual goal of Part Two) on the part of your hero?

> Tertia is abducted and drugged, and an attempt is made on her life by way of a near drowning. Alex finds her and saves her.

NOTES FROM LARRY: Good—if you can explain how killing her, while pregnant, serves the needs of the killer. If the baby also dies, does that mean the killer becomes the heir (meaning it must be Marc Antony)?

But I fear a major mistake forthcoming. Ultimately, Tertia needs to *save herself*. Do *not* rely on Alex to do the saving. We are rooting for her, not necessarily Alex. This is *her* story; *she* needs to defeat Antony and her husband.

This is a make-or-break issue. It's the difference between a "romance" that doesn't make dramatic sense and a mainstream book that could be stellar. She needs to earn the nametag of hero.

Do you have a *pinch point* moment in the *middle* of your Part Two sequence?

A Cassius POV scene where he and his mother devise a new plan on how to find Tertia.

NOTES FROM LARRY: And do what to her, or with her, specifically? The consequences of finding her is where the threat lies. The reader needs to know and feel the weight of that threat.

What is the Midpoint contextual shift/twist in your story? What new information does it impart to the story, and how does this shift the hero's context from "responder/wanderer" to "attacker/warrior?"

The attempt on Tertia's life ends in miscarriage. Believing Cassius orchestrated her near drowning, she realizes that even without the baby she still has the ammunition to be free of Cassius.

NOTES FROM LARRY: A good plot twist. But for it to work, the reader needs to *immediately* be able to root for a different outcome—it was about the child; now it's about Tertia's own safety, and not allowing these villains to win. This dynamic needs to be set up subtly in the exposition that precedes the midpoint.

An alliance by marriage is only good as long as the parties involved are alive. Cassius's attempt on her life is proof he holds no special regard for her family. Brutus will have to grant her a divorce, which will also force Cassius to return her dowry. (Worldbuilding fact: Divorce is only possible if a woman's patriarch or husband permits it. Tertia's patriarch is Brutus.)

NOTES FROM LARRY: Good. Then *this* becomes her heroic quest—to convince her brother to grant her this divorce on these grounds, and to avoid Cassius in the meantime. Is this credible? Have you put her in a position to pull this off? What equity does she have with her brother (that needs to be established; Brutus can't suddenly enter the story as a rabbi-out-of-the-tunic solution).

What happens in Part Three of your story, now that your hero is in proactive attack mode (against the *external* problem/goal)?

> Tertia learns from Alex how to wield a dagger in self-defense so as never to be taken by surprise again. She falls in love with Alex. She has sex with Alex. She gets her aunt on her side.

NOTES FROM LARRY: Careful ... we'll never swallow the notion that she could defeat Cassius in a knife fight. She'll need a better solution or strategy than this.

This is a very important part of the story: She needs to be on a path toward doing something specific to achieve her goal. She can't be passive here, simply responding to what comes at her (that was the context of the Part Two scenes). She needs to be proactive, in charge of her own fate, doing something ... and there needs to be continued obstacles and hazards in doing so.

What is your strategy to escalate dramatic tension, pace, and stakes in the second half of your story?

> Tertia's brother does not believe that Cassius was involved in her kidnapping or near drowning and her mother takes his side. Tertia turns to Alex, the only person who she thinks believes in her, and asks him to run away with her. He rejects her because he knows she will never be happy without the life that she knows or the family she loves. Cassius and Brutus discover the lovers together, and Tertia is forced to go east with Cassius as he begins to build an army, while Alex is imprisoned for sleeping with another man's wife.

NOTES FROM LARRY: It sounds like she's still in passive victim mode. What is her *plan*? Her strategy? At this point, you need to give the reader something to *root* for, not just a diary/documentary of hopeless helplessness.

What is the Second Plot Point in your story? How does this change or affect the hero's proactive role? What new information enters the story here?

On the brink of committing suicide because she thinks she'll never be free and never loved or valued, Tertia realizes that she isn't the one who has to die. If Cassius were dead, then she would be free.

NOTES FROM LARRY: Be careful—it's really hard to root for a hero who is considering suicide. But overall, *now* you're cooking. This is huge. It's a great second plot point. Love it.

But your Part Three quartile is still contextually off the mark, because she's victim-y, helpless, not really working an angle or a strategy there (in the scenes after the midpoint and before the Second Plot Point). It's okay if her plan tanks, but she needs to transition from "responder" (in Part Two) to "attacker" (in Part Three).

Do that, and show us how "all is lost" right before the Second Plot Point, and then *make* the Second Plot Point her moment of clarity—she has to *kill her husband.* Now you've got a killer Part Four and resolution on your hands.

I hope. It depends on how you end it. I'm on pins and needles here.

Your reader will be, too … if you tweak some of this, as I've described.

How does your story end? Describe how your hero becomes the primary catalyst for this resolution.

Tertia attempts to poison Cassius, but she fails.

NOTES FROM LARRY: Well, I hope there's more, a postscript of some kind that shows her *winning* in some way.

At the Battle of Phillippi, Tertia is imprisoned in Cassius's tent. When Cassius believes he is defeated, he returns to his tent to commit suicide, but he tells Tertia he is going to kill her first. Tertia knows she doesn't deserve to die. He might not find her worthy of living, but she does. Cassius lunges at her, and she uses the dagger Alex had given her to mortally stab Cassius before he can hurt her.

NOTES FROM LARRY: And there you go. *Nice!* I love it.

You have a potential winner on your hands. The key is understanding your own core dramatic arc, and including dramatic tension over the course of all four parts.

After reading this, I would toss the Alex POV. This isn't his story. It slows things down, and it's off topic. Use him as a catalyst, someone she falls for, but don't ask the reader to root for him from his point of view. It's not his story; it's hers.

If this was my story, I'd tell the *whole* thing from Tertia's POV. For one thing, that would simplify what could end up being a massively complex and confusing read.

Read *The Hunger Games*, which is entirely in Katniss's POV (unlike the movie, which goes behind the curtain) Your story doesn't benefit from including multiple points of view. Take us on Tertia's journey, and make us feel what she feels, fear what she fears, aspire to what she aspires to—in first person. That's the strategy I would recommend.

Notice, too, how the so-called "romance" angle virtually disappears in these answers. That's because it is a bit contrived and forced; it is *not* part of the core dramatic arc. So don't force the Alex romance, or if you do "feature" it, Alex needs a bigger role as co-conspirator. He can't disappear from the story as he does. They need to do this together—do it *for* each other. That'll make the romance angle work, without trying to turn the whole story into a "romance novel," which it isn't.

I hope these notes help take you to a higher level with this great story. I encourage you to write it with courage and vision, and not to please your genre-specific writer friends. This is bigger than that.

Thanks for the look. I wish you great success. Please keep me posted.

POSTSCRIPT NOTE FROM LARRY

I hope you can see why I included this case study. Even when a concept is terrific, full of promise, and dripping with innate dramatic tension, there can be a laundry list of ways to screw it up. The key to avoiding disaster is your level of storytelling knowledge, which contributes toward a heightened story sensibility that will serve you once you square off with the blank page.

Story sensibility is everything. It's the key to fulfilling your writing dreams. The lack of this sensibility may be what got you rejected, while nourishing it will empower you toward the successful revision of your story.

I hope you've found the tools and rationale to embark upon that journey in this book. Nothing will ever make the task of writing a great story easier, because the process is inherently fraught with risks and challenges, and is never an exact science. But those tools and truths will make the awaiting rewards more reachable, elevating you into a league that tolerates no poseurs and no guesswork.

The only other ingredient required, worth mentioning here, as you close the cover on this book, is *perseverance*. Story sensibility is an organic thing. It feeds on input and glories in practice. Feed it well, cultivate its growth, and learn to trust it as you move forward.

May you be the hero in your own writing story. May your quest be filled with bliss and your endings full of reward, the greatest of which is knowing you gave your story your all, and that your all was fueled by truth and the courage to embrace it.

INDEX

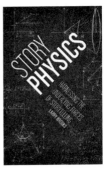